Fighting Soldier

★★★★★★★★★★★★★★★★★★★★★★★★★★★★★★★★★★★

Second Lieutenant Joseph Douglas Lawrence, twenty-three years old, France, 1918

★★★★★★★★★★★★★★★★★★★★★★★★★★★★★★★★★★★

★★★★★★★★★★★★★★★★★★★★★★★★★★★★★★★★★★

FIGHTING SOLDIER
The AEF in 1918

BY JOSEPH DOUGLAS LAWRENCE

edited by Robert H. Ferrell

COLORADO ASSOCIATED UNIVERSITY PRESS

★★★★★★★★★★★★★★★★★★★★★★★★★★★★★★★★★★

Published by Colorado Associated University Press
Boulder, Colorado 80309
International Standard Book Number 0-87081-158-4
Library of Congress Catalog Card Number 85-72233
Printed in the United States of America

*Publication of this book was made possible by a generous
grant from the Vanetta Rickards Betts Memorial Fund*

Colorado Associated University Press is a cooperative
publishing enterprise supported in part by Adams State
College, Colorado State University, Fort Lewis College,
Mesa College, Metropolitan State College, University of
Colorado, University of Northern Colorado, University
of Southern Colorado, and Western State College.

This book is dedicated to my father, Joseph Henry Lawrence, M.D. (U.S. Medical Corps), a conscientious man who inspired courage, truth, and patriotism

Contents

Illustrations

Maps

FOREWORD

This narrative of things that took place in 1918 has meaning for people of today; it is a part of history that should not be forgotten. When we entered both World Wars we were not prepared to engage a major nation. In both wars the men of other nations held the enemy until we could build a fighting force, which took considerable time. For them our unpreparedness brought grave danger. The Kaiser had just about won World War I when we entered. All over the war zone we soldiers were told we were too late, the war was lost. While watching a new British infantry company move up toward the front I heard an elderly English YMCA man standing near me say, "Look at those old men and young boys. What can you expect of them in battle?"

The allies won the war—fortunately America got a force into the field in the nick of time. For the United States, World War I was a citizens' war, fought by citizen soldiers who trained hurriedly. Men who loved their country were willing to die.

And so I pass on, to another generation, an account of patriotism and courage by Americans of long ago.

J.D.L.
Clemson, S.C.
Oct. 1, 1985

INTRODUCTION

The author of the memoir that follows was born on January 10, 1895, in Roanoke, Virginia, the son of Joseph H. and Mary Jones Lawrence. After graduating from high school in Florence, South Carolina, he worked as a bookkeeper at the State Bank of McBee until he enlisted in the army in 1917. After returning from World War I he attended the University of Virginia, where he studied mining engineering. In 1921 he left the university because of the difficult times—a depresson that lasted until 1922—and sought employment in the lead, zinc, and silver mines of the American West. His first job, as a laborer in an Oklahoma mine, offered a bare subsistence, and he left it to work in another mine in Kellogg, Idaho. En route he "hoboed" on passenger and freight trains, and his life took a few lively turns. Flushed off the engine tender of a passenger train at Columbus, Kansas, he outran the police and caught a freight train out of town. Arrested while sleeping under a railroad water tank at Grand Island, Nebraska, he was held on suspicion of robbing a bank the night before, but personal identification cleared him. He was put off a train again in Alliance, Nebraska. Upon reaching Kellogg he found employment with the Bunker Hill and Sullivan Mining and Concentrating Company, working as a mucker, loading cars 1,800 feet underground. He also braced drifts after ore was blasted to the floor. After much experience, and having saved a modest sum, he returned to South Carolina, where he operated lumber and lath mills. He then obtained a position in Atlanta as a bookkeeper and was employed by Ernst and Ernst, certified public accountants, and became a C.P.A.

In the 1930s, Lawrence joined the Federal Farm Board in Washington and then its successor, the Farm Credit Administration. In 1948 he returned to South Carolina to become president of the Columbia Bank for Cooperatives, from which he retired in 1961. During his years with the Columbia Bank he again spent time in Washington, on a leave of absence, with appointments to the Farm Credit Administration and as chairman of the board of directors and general manager of the Central Bank for Cooperatives. After retirement he organized development banks in Latin America and Thailand and established the Inter-American Cooperative Bank Development Program in Washington, under contracts with the government of Ecuador, the Agency for International Development, and the Cooperative League of the United States.

Lawrence has been a member of the board of directors of the Agricultural Hall of Fame and the Governor's Advisory Council for Agriculture in South Carolina, and presently belongs to the University Associates, a group that serves the University of South Carolina as a link between its president and the public.

He married Thelma Elizabeth Dellinger of Mount Holly, North Carolina, in 1923, and after her death in 1970 he married Mary Robertson Wyndham of Columbia. There were two children by the first marriage, Joseph D. Lawrence, Jr., of Houston, Texas, and Anna Marie Glenn of Columbia.

In the 1920s and 1930s, as Lawrence thought about his service in World War I and as the approach of World War II made his army experiences seem ever more memorable, he put together a typescript account for the enjoyment of his children and grandchildren. This was the origin of *Fighting Soldier*. In the 1970s, when many veterans of World War I were passing from the scene, or else removing to Florida or the Southwest or to California, or entering nursing homes, historians at the U.S. Army Military History Institute at Carlisle Barracks, Pennsylvania, sent out detailed questionnaires to the veterans about their military service and made a special appeal for photographs, letters, diaries, and written accounts; they placed the questionnaires, together with franked envelopes, in Veterans Administration mailings. Lawrence sent his typescript to Carlisle, and it was there that I found it. An inquiry directed to his address at that time, a South Carolina sea island with the quaint name of Frogmore, brought a quick response, we continued to correspond, and the result was a rewriting of the memoir and a division into chapters with introductions and notes, the latter gathered at the back. The present account is essentially the same as Lawrence's initial type-script, but without commentaries that would have dated his thoughts, and without introductory pages that pertained largely to his first months of service in South Carolina.

Fighting Soldier is a truly remarkable description of what war was like during the first great war of the present century. It is the story of a common soldier, eventually a second lieutenant. It is one of the best, perhaps even *the* best, of all the memoirs in the World War I files of personal papers, now some seven thousand, stored in the Military History Research Collection at Carlisle.

★ I ★
GETTING "OVER THERE"

Joseph Douglas Lawrence in June 1917 enlisted in a National Guard company based in Florence, South Carolina, where he formerly had lived and had friends. The company entered federal service in July, assembled at Florence, pitched its tents on the grounds of the Central Public School, and in August entrained for Camp Sevier, near Greenville, where troops of South Carolina, North Carolina, and Tennessee were reorganized into the 30th Division.[1]

To set out what happened to Lawrence thereafter would be in some ways to repeat the experience of hundreds of thousands of his countrymen. The 30th Division spent all winter at Sevier, a very unpleasant place because of the inclement weather. It was the coldest winter in many years, with driving winds, heavy rains, and snow on the ground for weeks. The men shivered in their tents. The little Sibley stoves provided by army quartermasters were almost no help, for at the tops of the stovepipes the spark arresters clogged and the resultant fires set tents ablaze. Lawrence and his friends slept in their clothes for the entire winter.

In addition to the weather there was the often senseless routine. Lawrence's friend Lieutenant Sam

Royall, later historian of the 118th Infantry Regiment, remembered how "the drills, hikes, trench work and other forms of amusement continued through many weary long months. Day after day the men struggled through eight hours of work, slowly but steadily progressing toward a standard that would mark them trained soldiers." The routines only annoyed the men. "In the humble opinion of the author, a little less work and a little more freedom would have accomplished the same result in a less time. . . . At the end of four months of this constant grind, the men grew stale, or, in the slang of a soldier, more than fed up, and began to recede instead of continuing to improve. The ultimate object of all this was to inculcate a stern discipline, yet when we were placed in the trenches, a great deal of this discipline was of necessity relaxed. If the Australians had any superiors as fighters, we never came into contact with them, yet the discipline among these famous troops was a joke judging by the system laid down for Americans. The author sincerely believes that a lot of the time spent in this training was an absolute waste of time insofar as it affected the actual fighting in which we participated."[2]

During this period the larger scene, national and international, was hardly apparent to the newly inducted soldiers. Beyond a few evidences in camp, such as the initial lack of uniforms and rifles, Lawrence could not sense that a near chaos had enveloped the War Department in Washington, that expansion of the army was proving extremely difficult. Officers in Washington had never experienced such sudden requirements. The peacetime army had never before brought men together in a unit as large as a World War I division. Indeed, such a division was larger than the entire U.S. army at the turn of the present century.

Overseas the American Expeditionary Forces, the AEF, commanded by General John J. Pershing, grew very slowly. By September 1917 the AEF was only 61,531 strong. By the spring of 1918, Pershing had received only four divisions. These troops he then had to train. The AEF's commander established schools for officers of each of his divisions, who instructed the men in elementary principles of machine guns, mortars, and gas warfare. Officers also trained men in construction and maintenance of trenches and other points of warfare as practiced on the Western Front.

At long last, in May 1918, the AEF began to receive its divisions. Hundreds of thousands of American troops streamed into French ports: in May 245,945; June, 278,664; July, 306,350; August, 285,974; September, 257,457. By the time of the armistice in November 1918 the AEF had grown to forty-two divisions, a huge addition to Allied forces—more troops in France than were in the British Expeditionary Force, almost more than the French had mobilized in their own country. It was in the nick of time, for the collapse of the Russian front in November 1917, after the Russian Revolution, had opened an opportunity for the German army to shift divisions from east to west and gain the advantage on the Western Front in the war's fourth year. Between March and July 1918 the Germans launched five massive offensives against Allied lines in hope of breaking through before the Americans could arrive.

Douglas Lawrence's 30th Division began the move overseas early in May. About 9:00 A.M., May 4, 1918, Lawrence's company marched down the regimental street to the railroad a mile away, 250 men led by the band playing "Over There." Sixty-seven years later Lawrence can still remember the first sergeant of the company, Fred Sexton, his best friend in the army, at the head of the column. Sexton was killed in the Argonne.

The trip to France passed in a whirl—the three-day train journey to New York and thence to Camp Mills on Long Island, then back to Hoboken and the Cunard liner Orduna. *On May 11, 1918, the* Orduna *sailed down the harbor and out to sea, joining a convoy of two other transports, with a Canadian converted cruiser out in front and an American cruiser bringing up the rear. The twelve-day trip was a nightmare, with bad quarters, terrible food, and much seasickness. The officers ensconced themselves in staterooms on the top decks and abandoned the men to the fetid holds, and day after day the mess lines wound through corridors and up and down stairs, men resentful of their condition yet unable to remedy it. Afterward came a quick trip by train across southern England from Liverpool to Dover, to take the steamer to Calais.*

France proved little more attractive than the voyage overseas. Lawrence spent some time in a rest camp on the outskirts of Calais, marching everywhere in full pack, a backbreaking experience. For a short while thereafter his company was billeted, to use the French word, in a village of thirty or forty farmhouses. It moved to another village, Tournehem, close to the front in Flanders, which unlike the preceding one Lawrence remembered by name. There on dark nights the Americans saw a glow from gun flashes and heard a low rumble and on some nights the rumble grew to a roar when the infantry engaged. Then came a long, agonizing march into Belgium.

Belgium, heroic little country, devastated, yet game to the last—the term "fighting to the last ditch" certainly applied to the little Belgian army that was still carrying on, stretched now across a small corner of Flanders. The territory held by the Belgians and their British allies when we entered Belgium was so small that we marched across it in six hours. Half the time we were under range of German artillery in country that was uninhabitable for noncombatants and not very comfortable for soldiers.

We had left Tournehem in the usual way—the distance was long and we therefore marched. July 2, early, we had assembled, and of all the marches I think this one was the most severe. The easy life in Tournehem had softened us, the weather was hot, and the rate of march too fast. Again the heavy equipment added to the hardship. After we began the other battalions of the 118th Infantry joined us, and then the other regiments of the division, except for artillery, so practically the entire division was on the march. We got along fine until about noon when the men became fatigued. We did not halt for the midday meal. Shortly after noon we saw a sizable town in the distance and felt sure we would stop, but we passed through without a halt, crossed a river on the far side of the town, and then beheld the steepest, longest hill I have ever seen, before or since. The column pushed right on up, and here the trouble began, for we were nearly exhausted, the heat was terrific, our canteens empty, and packs and other equipment bore down like lead.

That hill was a terror. Shortly after we started up, the weaker members of the column began to fall out and drop in their tracks, and others followed, until it looked like the whole column would drop on the roadside. The officers and sergeants drove as many men back into the

5

Northwestern France and southwestern Belgium

column as they could with a combination of oaths and pleas. Orders came from the brigade commander, Brigadier General L. D. Tyson, to keep the men in column by all means. The general was riding in an automobile.³ I recall the case of old "Steamboat," who in loud tones told the officers to go to hell, that he wasn't going to walk up that damned hill. A sergeant stretched Steamboat out on the road with a blow of his fist between Steamboat's eyes, and then fixed a bayonet and with several jabs forced Steamboat to his feet and up the hill. It took all the strength I had to hold out until we reached the top, but I managed it.

Even after we reached the top the column continued at the same fast pace and after covering about two miles came to a halt on the side of the road in the blazing sun without shade of any kind. The halt lasted for about half an hour, during which time we ate our lunch. Again we were in motion, and soon our regained strength was disappearing in the hot sun and the rate of march. Men began dropping. We would see villages ahead and feel sure we would halt, but swung into and out of village after village. In the middle of the afternoon we had about reached the limit of endurance, but not so. On and on, villages, forests, down the white gravel roads. Whole squads straggled. One corporal straggled from the line with his seven men and fell on the grass by the road, and was promptly accosted by an English officer, riding a horse, and ridiculed. The corporal jumped to his feet, drew his bayonet, and said, "Go to hell, you son of a bitch, or I'll run this bayonet through you!" The Englishman rode on, as well he should have. By 5:00 P.M. our company was reduced to about a third, bent double with heavy packs, dragging their feet as if they were lead weights. The sergeants and officers were at the rear of the company now, driving the men, themselves about exhausted. Toward the last Sergeant Brud Segars of Jefferson turned to me and said, "Lawrence, I have gone as far as I can. Let's drop out and tell 'em to go to hell." I replied that I would if they did not halt at the next bend in the road that we could see about three-quarters of a mile ahead. We reached the bend without a halt, but then could see in the distance a village that we thought might be our destination, and so decided to hang on. Sure enough, we halted near the village, Rubrouck, close to the Belgian border.

We actually had not stopped in the village but on the other side, where we turned into the fields with about a third of the men in column. The others straggled in during the night. Both my feet were a mass of burst blisters, and I was bent double with my heavy pack, holding my rifle by the muzzle with the stock trailing in the dirt. We pitched the pup tents and lined up for supper.

The British had prepared the supper, and if ever insult was added to injury it was done here. We each received a small piece of rabbit, along with a cup of sugarless tea. I know that King George's ears must have burned from what we had to say about him and his army.

After this so-called meal we returned to our pup tents, took our blankets and extra clothes, keeping only those we had on, and with our other things that we did not need carried them off some distance and buried them, determined to march light the next day. During the night the regimental officers observed the natives of the village wearing American uniforms and in possession of various kinds of American equipment. They made an investigation and found that practically all the men had thrown away everything but their guns, the clothes they wore, and their overcoats—which they used to sleep under. This was a serious offense, but they could not

8

Brigadier General Lawrence D. Tyson and his automobile

court-martial one of us without including the whole regiment, so the matter was dropped and an attempt made to find the discarded equipment, which met with very little success.

After a good night's rest the march started again and was hard, but we did not suffer as we did the day before. That night we halted near Herzeele, two or three miles from the Belgian border, and not caring to take a chance on more English rabbit we scattered among the nearby farmhouses and managed to buy a few eggs. We found we could not use our "French" here, as the people seemed to speak another language that we denominated Belgian. We were billeted in barns and went to sleep to the roar of the big guns that sounded very close.

On the morning of July 4, 1918, the 30th Division crossed into Belgium, the first Americans to enter. Our crossing happily was with each company in inverted

The march into Belgium

order, that is, the short-legged squad led the column, with the number-one squad of the tallest company members bringing up the rear. Each company of the battalion adopted the same formation, which gave the short fellows a chance, as they set the pace and the long legs in the rear had to conform. We moved swiftly, however, for it seemed we were needed immediately on the front.

We passed through a town of size, Watou, one of the two localities in Belgium not in the hands of the Germans that had not been deserted by its inhabitants. At times it was under shellfire. In the town I saw my first French troops in marching column, long columns of infantry going we did not know where. The town was alive with moving troops—American, English, Scotch Highlanders in kilts, French, Belgians; evidently the Allies were expecting something to happen in the neighborhood. A few miles after Watou we saw huge shell craters, British reserve troops in camp, field hospitals with ambulances moving about, big guns mounted on flatcars, airplanes flying above, the big sausage-like observation balloons of both the British and Germans. There was the increasing roar of the artillery, and in early afternoon we came under shellfire for the first time, the shells whining overhead and bursting in adjoining fields. The command was given to march in column of twos in platoon units, with intervals between platoons of about twenty-five yards. Shelling became heavier, and command for double time was given, and we trotted mile after mile in the hot July sun, and as we reached more exposed positions the platoons were broken into squads, trotting in column of twos. The men behaved well; I think the shelling helped the column move swiftly, even though the men realized their fatigue.

11

We passed through the shelled area in about three hours and did not halt; none of the men fell out.

Late in the afternoon we came to a camp known as Dirty Bucket Corner, four miles from the town of Ypres. Dirty Bucket Corner and Hell Fire Corner, which was nearby, were famous for the bloody struggles between the British and Germans waged at those places since the beginning of the war. It was here apparently that the Allies were expecting a big German push; it was for this reason that we were rushed to the sector. The Germans were massing troops and munitions, a sign of a big drive.

★ II ★
YPRES

The city of the cloth merchants of medieval times bore a name that in French was pronounced "Eee-pr" but in Anglo-American became "Wipers." Not much was left of it by the summer of 1918. During the nearly four years before the Americans arrived, the British and German armies had fought three battles at Ypres. In the first, at the beginning of the war in 1914, the German army had sought to wrest the Channel ports from the Allies; in the first days and weeks of the war everything seemed swirling chaos, but a front had formed from Nieuwpoort that included Ypres as one of its strongest points. In 1915 the Germans tried a new tactic of warfare on the Western Front, and chose Ypres for the momentous experiment; one day in April they sent over the lines a cloud of greenish vapor that a gentle breeze wafted toward the Allied trenches—chlorine gas, which choked and asphyxiated with horrible effect. French troops north of Ypres broke and fled, and the Canadians saved Ypres in a stand that was nothing short of heroic. In the Third Battle of Ypres in 1917, desperate fighting for the little town to the east of the city, Passchendaele, lent the locality's name not merely to the horrors of the local scene but to the entire series of engagements that the British army fought that year along the Somme.

The sheer desolation surrounding this fought-over area, the tragedy that it represented, was omnipresent—impossible for the Americans to forget. And yet Lawrence's regiment, while hardly lighthearted about being assigned to such a place, looked upon Ypres as an opportunity for instruction in modern war. The men afterward spoke of the months of "grade school" at Camp Sevier and of "high school" with the British at Ypres.[1]

At Ypres the men of the 30th Division learned about trenches. Trench warfare had developed on the Western Front nearly four years before when in August 1914 the opposing armies failed to reach a decision. Its beginning usually is dated from the war's second month, September, when the German VII Reserve Corps blocked the advance of the British I Corps on the Chemin des Dames ridge to the north of Soissons, a small city northeast of Paris. Within a few weeks the stalemate begun there had spread up and down the entire battle line, from Nieuwpoort all the way to Switzerland.

The Ypres salient, into which Lawrence's division had marched, contained some of the worst trenches—that is, the most uncomfortable—on the entire Western Front. The ground itself was low and marshy, like much of the land in Belgium. But at Ypres there seemed to be more rain than anywhere else along the Allied line. Here rain was an enemy almost worse than the Germans. It could descend at any time. Between October 25, 1914, and March 10, 1915, there were only eighteen dry days. In March 1916 the rainfall was the heaviest in thirty-five years. Nor did summer bring a respite. In July 1916 an officer wrote home: "The mud

Ruins of Cloth Hall and Cathedral, Ypres

is awful. Have had two days of torrential rain which has flooded everything." In 1917, at the height of the Third Battle of Ypres, a drizzle commenced on July 30 that continued without pause for the entire month of August.[2]

In the summer of 1918, Lawrence could not immediately comprehend the full discomforts of the Ypres salient. That was possible only over a period of several months. Meanwhile he found his introduction to trench warfare interesting because it allowed him to become acquainted with the British army.

I have never seen or heard of such an elaborate, complete line of defense as the British had built at this point. There was a trench with dugouts every three hundred yards from the front line in Ypres back four miles to and including Dirty Bucket. Everything was fronted with barbed wire and other entanglements. Artillery was concealed everywhere. Railroad tracks, narrow and standard gauge, reached from the trenches back into the zone of supply. Nothing had been neglected to hold this line, save only one important thing, enthusiasm among the troops, and that was the purpose of our presence.[3] General Pershing reluctantly had placed the 27th and 30th Divisions under command of the British. The big push never materialized, and probably our presence in the area had something to do with the Germans' change of mind.

Our camp at Dirty Bucket was in a grove of oak trees where there were enough huts built by the British to house the whole company, peaked roof affairs with the roofs extending to the ground—in fact they were all roof. Each hut was large enough for about fifteen men, and we slept on the floors without cots or bunks. Close by our camp were several still-occupied farmhouses, the occupants of which had refused to move, even though within range of German guns. These people were very unfriendly and would not let us get water from their wells.

It was during our several weeks in Dirty Bucket that, having transferred from supply to the line, I got down to hard work to learn the many things a line sergeant needed to know, things I could not learn while a supply sergeant, such matters as poison gas and trench raiding, the latter being practiced in the British reserve trenches nearby. The trenches were in the open and we had to be careful not to attract attention from the German observation balloons, a problem that helped the training.

All of our stay at Dirty Bucket was not spent in work, for we had some time for recreation, and it was during a recreation period that Steamboat Boggs and Slim Sowell had their famous fight.[4] These two worthies were noted for their weakness physically, and for lack of better amusement the boys of Company I staged the fight. After quite a bit of persuasion Steamboat and Slim embraced, and the struggle lasted for an hour or more, without either suffering as much as a scratch. They were both loud in their remarks and spent their energy, mental and physical, in this way. The fight went along nicely and was enjoyed by the audience until several English soldiers chanced by, saw the two men lying on the ground, clasped in each other's arms, apparently exhausted except for a few lazy motions of their feet and somewhat more action from their tongues. The Englishmen were horrified at what they called "a beastly show of brutality." One Englishman said, "The poor blokes have beat each other insensible." They proceeded to break up the fight, thereby nearly starting a real fight. The American spectators threatened them, called them numerous names, and warned them to "get going," which—being in the minority—they did.

After being in Dirty Bucket Camp for about ten days I had my first glimpse of the front-line trenches and for the first time heard bullets aimed in my direction. Officers and sergeants were being sent in small details to the front line for observation and a gentle baptism of fire, and I was assigned to go with a lieutenant from another company, a nice, agreeable fellow. We assembled about two hours before dark—eight men and officers—and climbed into a lorry and started the twelve or so miles to the front-line trenches. The road was roughly paved and shell craters made it worse. Fortunately, and like the French roads, it was lined with tall trees that hid the road, making it possible for us to travel in daylight without being seen from the sausage balloons.

After about three miles the shells began falling closer and things were a little uncomfortable. A big one landed in a nearby field, exploded with a mighty roar, and sent fragments flying through the treetops over our heads. A few seconds afterward our lorry ran under a low-hanging limb and the brushing of the leaves on top of the lorry sounded exactly like the rush of a shell through the air. We all gave up, thought we were done for; every man in that lorry thought he was dead.

After an hour's ride and just about dusk we came into Ypres, or what was left. The British held the town but that was all; it had been nearly destroyed by shellfire; there was not a building with a roof and few with four walls. The defending trenches skirted the town and in some places ran through outlying parts; here the British line formed a salient, horseshoe fashion, into the German line. Ypres was the scene of some of the bloodiest battles of the war. It was in Ypres that the Germans first used poison gas, with deadly effect, against the Canadians. As we rode into this shattered little city under cover of shadows of the approaching night, it seemed to me that the place was infested with numberless ghosts. The moon had risen enough for the ghostlike, leafless trees lining the banks of the black, sluggish Ijser River to cast the shadows of their broken and splintered limbs over this morbid stream that was the grave of so many British soldiers. Brick walls, single, without support, towered at dangerous angles; church steeples stood alone, the main parts of the churches blown away; chimneys without houses: all this was silhouetted against the sky, adding to the weird scene. Also weird was the large cemetery with every grave turned to a shell crater, every tombstone broken or blown off its base, shrubbery uprooted, all monuments shattered save for one large image of Christ untouched in the sea of destruction.

Our lorry came to a halt and we unloaded, and as we observed the scene we spoke not a word. The only sound was the hissing shells overhead, the ringing barks of British batteries as they fired in return. While we stood waiting for a guide, a battery opened with a terrific crash not twenty-five yards from where we were standing, and we were nearly swept off our feet by the detonation. We did not know the thing was there.

Our guide came and directed us to the ruins of a church where we boarded a little narrow-gauge train used for transporting supplies up to the trenches. The cars were about the size of a baby bed and drawn by a gasoline motor built on the order of the motor of an electric train. In this conveyance we rode about a mile as the crow flies, but three miles as the track went its tortuous course, and got off about a hundred yards in

19

the rear of the third-line trenches, known as the reserve trenches. We walked through the communication trenches leading to the second-line or support trenches and thence to the first-line trenches, which we did not enter but instead reported to the British officer commanding, who was in his headquarters, a large dugout a few yards behind the first line.

The officer greeted us in a friendly way and told the American lieutenant he was to remain with him and told his orderly to direct me to the sergeant-major's dugout via a winding, rough path along which I saw a few battered and twisted tree trunks standing out in the moonlight and flares shooting into the sky like so many roman candles. Our position seemed circumscribed by lights, because the lights were coming from the German trenches and the British lines were in the shape of a horseshoe.

Reaching the sergeant-major's dugout I was ushered in and presented to this worthy—a British sergeant-major is a high-ranking individual, chiefly in his own estimation and to a somewhat lesser degree to the men under him. He received me with the remark that I could bloody well see all of the trenches that I wanted without bothering him. He was a powerfully built man, broad-shouldered, with a head of short, bristling hair. He spoke with a terrible cockney brogue, and after the orderly left he pointed to a makeshift bunk in a dark corner of the dugout and said, "There's your bunk, Sammy. Sleep while you can and see the bloody trenches when you 'ave to." With that he crawled in his bunk and went instantly to sleep.

What to do? A British sergeant-major is a high-ranking individual, as mentioned, and has more authority than our first sergeants. He has an orderly, sometimes two, and as a rule he has more influence with the men than do their immediate officers. I sat on my bunk and wondered what to do; I did not want to argue with His Royal Highness, especially if I had to wake him. There was a soldier in the dugout sitting at a small table on which dimly burned a candle, the only light, and I went over to him and explained that I had come up to get a glimpse of trench warfare and understood I was to spend the night in the trenches with combat soldiers. He replied: "You had better do what the major says. You'll be bloody-well fed up on the trenches before the bloomin' war is over." Then he added in encouragement: "If nothing else will suit you, I will take you for a round after the major wakes up tomorrow." Realizing this was the best I could do, I followed the major's example and soon went to sleep, but was awakened by a detail entering the dugout to report a skirmish with a German patrol in which one English soldier was killed. The major resented being wakened, but took the report, gave a few orders, and turned over on his bunk with the remark, "Poor Bill, 'e's gone West where a lot of good blokes 'as gone before 'im." He went to sleep. I did not get to sleep right away but thought of the soldier just killed and listened to a monotonous song of the orderly that went something like this: "Damn 'im, 'e's a cousin of mine and a member of the German band." This seemed to be the whole song, and he repeated it hundreds of times before I went to sleep.

Once again before morning I was awakened by a patrol entering the dugout, and this time it was to report about going into no-man's-land to repair barbed wire entanglements. The detail was in charge of a powerful black-haired sergeant, pleasant-faced and agreeable, who said they unexpectedly had met another patrol in no-man's-land, and upon being challenged with the customary "Who goes there?" a member of the other patrol replied, "First, Fifth, York, and Lancasters." This part of the sergeant's report brought an outburst from the sergeant-major, who stormed, "What the bloody 'ell did the fool mean telling who he was? I suppose 'e wanted to tell Jerry 'is whole 'ist'ry. If I'd been there I'd shot the bloody fool. 'ow the 'ell does 'is Majesty expect us to win the war when 'e sends us blokes like that?" It seemed to me that he was making a lot out of an incident, but he settled down in a few minutes, crawled back on his bunk, and went to sleep. The sergeant and detail stayed for quite a while, drinking hot tea and talking. After they left, the sergeant-major's orderly came over and asked if I did not want tea, and I decided I would like some, so got up and drank several cups. He appeared more friendly and we talked. He was interested in America and knew some of the latest American songs. He said he thought the names in America were the prettiest in the world, and named Tennessee, Kentucky, Chesapeake, Indiana, California. We talked for about an hour and then decided to follow the sergeant-major's example and get some sleep.

I was awakened next morning by voices in the dugout, for a lieutenant was talking to the orderly. It seemed he wanted to talk to the sergeant-major, but the sergeant-major appeared to be asleep and the orderly didn't want to wake him.

"But I must see him, my man," said the officer.

"I wouldn't wake the major," replied the orderly. " 'e's had a hard night, sir."

"But it is important and I have no time to waste," said the officer.

"If you wake 'im, 'e will be in a bad humor," argued the orderly, who appeared to be in an uncomfortable situation. It was evident that both the lieutenant and the orderly feared the sergeant-major's wrath. I was surprised, as the English army was noted for its discipline and, I thought, maintained a strict line of differences between officers and men. It appeared that the sergeant-major was boss in this locality.

The lieutenant walked back and forth impatiently, muttering that he must see the sergeant-major. Suddenly he spied me and said, "I say, orderly, who is this man asleep over there?"

The orderly replied, " 'e is a Yankee that came up 'ere to see the war."

After pacing back and forth for a minute or two the lieutenant said, "I am going to wake him. I must go." With that he punched the sergeant-major in the ribs with his cane.

The sergeant-major woke instantly. I think he was awake all the time. With a roar and the customary English oath with a lot of "bloody's" and not much of anything else he growled out, "Who the 'ell's punching me with 'is bloody stick? Can't you let a man rest 'at's 'ad a 'ard night?" With that remark he turned over and covered up his head.

The lieutenant stalked out of the dugout with the remark, "That's a bloody poor way for a sergeant-major to treat an officer."

I slept until about 10:00 A.M., when I got up and had breakfast of corned beef and tea with the orderly, and while we were eating the sergeant-major woke up and joined us. After we were through he sent for a soldier to come and take me into the trenches. I was delighted. We went out of the dugout, which I found to be on the lee of a small hill just a few yards behind the trenches. In this particular spot the trench was dug in because of the hill, but most of the trench that I went over that morning was in low ground.

This front-line trench in Belgium was a fascinating place. Most of Belgium is low ground, and it is impossible to dig for more than two to four feet on account of water. The trenches were dug to that depth and built up in front with sandbags. They were more breastworks than trenches. Their floors were covered with duckboard that kept the soldiers' feet dry, at least in dry weather, but if it rained the water would rise above the duckboards and even above the fire steps on which soldiers stood when firing or standing-to. We walked over a section of trench, past soldiers loitering on the fire step or sleeping in shallow dugouts in the back wall of the trench, and came to a place where we could look into no-man's-land without much danger of being seen by the enemy. The German trench was supposed to be five hundred yards away, and the Englishman pointed out ruins of buildings he thought were just behind the enemy front line. Suddenly he said, "Look, there's a Jerry!" I looked but was too late; the German had ducked out of sight. From this point we went to a pillbox, a concrete machine-gun nest, where the four-man crew greeted me warmly and explained the operation of their gun and gave me cigarettes and hot tea. Incidentally, it was on this trench tour that I first learned to smoke; cigarettes were offered to me so much by the English soldiers that I could not well refuse them.

After ten or fifteen minutes in the pillbox we returned to the sergeant-major's dugout, and he was asleep as usual. Lacking something better to do, I crawled on my bunk and went to sleep. Indeed, I slept so much while on this tour of observation that I lost all track of time. The dugout was dark and lighted at all times with a candle or two, and I did not know day from night. I would eat a while, drink tea and smoke, talk with the

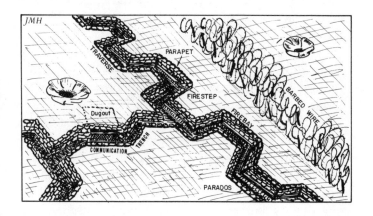

Trench warfare

orderly, and take a nap. As far as I could see, the sergeant-major slept all the time, although the orderly said he made tours of the trenches occupied by his men each night.

In this way my life passed in the trenches, on observation, with occasional moments of amusement— as when I was fortunate enough to observe a trench mortar in action.

The trench mortar experience came about because after becoming weary of sleeping and drinking tea I obtained permission of the sergeant-major to step outside the dugout for a few minutes. Behind the trenches here, built up with sandbags, the ground fell away slightly and one could walk along without being seen from the German lines. The section of trench where I was ran through the premises of what appeared to have been a country house of size, but all that was left were scattered heaps of bricks and mortar dust. Short, battered sections of stone wall showed that the house and garden had been enclosed. Splintered trunks of large trees showed where the front yard or lawn had been. While looking at this scene of destruction I then received my invitation to the trench mortar exhibition; an English soldier interrupted me with the news: "Go down and look 'er over Sammy," said he. "She's going to blow up one of Jerry's machine-gun nests we located in no-man's-land."

The mortar was in a small sandbag enclosure about six feet high, directly behind the trenches and therefore protected from German eyes. A trench mortar is a crude-looking affair used for dropping shells in trenches or on machine-gun nests, and I suppose it would be called a gun. The trajectory of its projectile is in the shape of an inverted U. This particular gun was about four feet long, four inches in diameter, and looked like the carbonic gas tubes used in soda fountains, with one of the rounded ends sawed off. The sawed-off end was the muzzle. The gun was set at an angle of about eighty-five degrees from horizontal, and its rounded end was seated in an iron plate about two feet square. The gun was fired by dropping a shell in the muzzle. The shell struck a plunger in the bottom and returned promptly—so promptly that the gunner hardly had time to get his hands out of the way.

Shortly after I arrived on the spot the gun crew commenced firing. There were two soldiers—one mature man, short of stature, and one boy about sixteen years old, possibly younger. The boy appeared nervous, and his older companion frequently scolded him. I could follow the shell with my eye as it left the mortar's muzzle, went high into the air, then turned and dropped on or about the spot where the machine gun was supposed to be. Shell after shell went up, and struck and exploded with a roar, scattering dust and debris high in the air. It appeared that the mortar crew had a certain number of shells to fire and could not leave until they fired them.

Evidently the shells were reaching their mark, as the German artillery responded almost immediately and with uncanny accuracy as to the position of the trench mortar. The first shell hissed directly over our heads and exploded a hundred yards behind. But for our sheltered position it would have been a direct hit. Other shells followed in quick succession but could not reach us in our sheltered position, although they came uncomfortably close and fragments flew all around us. When the shelling began the mortar crew worked frantically to get through and get away. The boy was all unstrung and crying bitterly. The man was setting the fuses and passing the shells to the boy to drop in the muzzle of the gun. The boy was so nervous that I expected to see his head blown off any second. His companion swore and coaxed but was nervous himself. I preferred to be somewhere else but did not want to run while the Tommy that directed me there stood by nonchalantly. He probably would have enjoyed seeing me run.

I felt sorry for the boy; the war was hard enough on able-bodied men but terrible on boys and old men. To have to stand and face fear is an awful thing, and this was what the little Tommy was having to do. I saw him drop a shell into the muzzle of the mortar and jump back. The shell did not come out as expected; sometimes they do not fire immediately but remain in the gun a few seconds and then fire, usually knocking the head or arm off the gunner trying to locate the trouble. When the shell stuck, the man swore at the boy. They managed to get the thing fired. Meanwhile Jerry dropped his shells faster and closer. While I stood there wondering if I had not better clear out, the sergeant-major's orderly came running and said the major wanted me to come into the dugout at once. When I entered he greeted me with, "Stay in this dugout, Sammy. You'll get hurt out there, and then I will have to apologize to President Wilson."

When I left the trench mortar the gunners were striving frantically to fire their quota of shells before Jerry blew them to bits. Back in the dugout, with nothing else to do, I crawled on the bunk and went to sleep.

I was awakened by a messenger who said I was to join the American lieutenant, who was preparing to leave to rejoin the Americans. I packed, bade the sergeant-major and orderly goodby, and joined the lieutenant. He too was ready to travel, so we set out down the communication trenches toward the rear, guided by a Tommy. We went to some kind of headquarters and waited a half hour or more, for what reason I do not know. While waiting I was approached by an English soldier, a mere boy, with a cup of hot chocolate in his hand. "'ere Sammy, drink this. It'll make you feel better," he grinned, as he handed me the chocolate. He was right; it did make me feel better, considerably so, since I had left the dugout just before mealtime and was hungry. I always found the English big-hearted and generous with what little they had. While we were on the march I have had them give me sandwiches and hot tea. I found them likable fellows and was sorry when I left their area.

When we left the headquarters it was almost dark, and we walked a distance to a railhead where we waited an hour or more for a ration train on which to ride back. While we were waiting, two litter bearers passed with a dead soldier, killed that day. As they passed, the soldiers standing around the railhead all snapped to attention—the rule in the British army is to salute all processions bearing the dead.

Several hours after dark the ration train eased up and was quietly and quickly unloaded, and as quietly loaded with articles going to the rear. We crawled on, and I climbed on top of a car loaded with some kind of hard material covered with a tarpaulin. I perched on top with my rifle and pack and held on as best I could. The lieutenant got on the next car. We moved slowly through the darkness, without light of any kind, into the outskirts of Ypres. The track ran through the ruins of a church that we could dimly make out in the inky darkness. At this point the shelling began to get heavy and we stayed in the ruined church several hours, and I got very tired sitting in my uncomfortable position. We could only sit and wait, and could not smoke, as lights of any kind were forbidden. After a while the shelling died down and our little train got into motion and ran slowly for a while and then began gaining speed. Too much, I thought, for the darkness was broken by no light of any kind. The swaying motion of the car made me sleepy and I began to nod. Suddenly there was a loud crash, a terrible jolt, and I was thrown into the air clear of the car and fell into a deep ditch on the side of the track. I was stunned for a moment, not knowing what had happened. I thought we had been struck by a shell. My arm was badly wrenched. I sat up and could hear angry voices arguing above me, groped around and found my rifle, and struggled to the track to see what had happened, only to find that we had had a head-on collision with another train.

Long after midnight we reached Dirty Bucket, and we unloaded and the lieutenant went one way and I the other. I did not know how to find our camp, but after wandering I saw familiar landmarks and found the hut in which I was billeted when I left, crawled in among the sleeping forms, and was soon asleep. Next morning my friends greeted me and I took up the routine I had left a few days before. I learned I had been away three days; I had lost all account of time.

Two or three days later it was my turn to go into the line again. Moving back through Ypres, and into the trenches, this time with two squads of the third platoon in my charge, I reported to an English sergeant named Walley, of the York and Lancaster Regiment, who said he was expecting us and would place my men for me. He led us into a deep trench floored with duckboards and apparently in good condition all round, and it seemed already well manned with English soldiers. He placed my men, one between two of his own, so the trench was manned with Americans in every alternate position.

Everything seemed to be repeating itself. After many warnings that not a sound was to be made, nothing done to attract Jerry in any way, the sergeant turned from the men to me and said I was to stay with him in his dugout. Another dugout! I thought I had had enough. But then I thought I had better do as the sergeant said, as my instructions were to do as the English told us.

When we turned to go to the dugout Sergeant Walley said, "Hi say, sergeant, where's your orderly?"

I informed him that American sergeants did not have orderlies.

He was astonished. "You 'ave to 'ave an orderly, sergeant. Detail a man. You 'ave to 'ave a cooker. You can't take the time to cook yourself."

One of my men, overhearing the conversation, said, "Let me have the job, sergeant. I will be your orderly. I would rather do that than stay out here in this damn ditch." I said, "All right, but remember, you do not have to."

We retired to Walley's dugout, across a paved road from the trench in which my men were stationed. The road ran through the three lines of trenches and as I found out later was a dangerous spot; we had to be mighty careful how we crossed from the trench to the dugout and back. After we reached the dugout Walley had my "orderly" and his orderly prepare a meal that tasted good to me and to my acting orderly, who appeared pleased with the arrangement.

Walley discussed trench warfare, telling of the many fights he had been in, and showed a scar on his shoulder where a German had shot him in a hand-to-hand encounter. He said the German shot him with a pistol, but he immediately, he said, killed the German with his bayonet.

31

We slept until time to stand-to, when we took positions with our men, with the orderlies left in the dugout. German artillery fired on the trenches in the early morning as usual, but there were no casualties. After the firing died down the men were allowed to loiter and sleep in the dugouts at the rear of the trench. We went through the same procedure the next night.

Early the following morning Walley said he had orders to take a raiding party to the German trench and try to capture one or more prisoners so the British and Americans would know what units were occupying the trench in front of us. He said I could go, and I told him I would. He began to instruct me in what to do, but before the appointed hour a messenger arrived with orders to report to Captain Gillespie with my detail.[5] The messenger said he thought we Americans were to take over a section of the front-line trenches.

★ III ★
LOST IN NO-MAN'S-LAND

The 30th Division had been brought up in anticipation of a German attack at Ypres, and Lawrence's regiment, the 118th Infantry, was assigned—in case of trouble— a sector of the East Poperinghe trench system, generally known as the Blue Line. The regimental sector was about 2,000 yards long, and joined the Belgians on the left and the 117th Infantry Regiment (which together with the 118th constituted the 59th Infantry Brigade of the 30th Division) on the right. The East Poperinghe system covered the main road from Poperinghe to Elverdinghe. It was strongly fortified by barbed wire, trenches, and concrete dugouts and had a well-defined field of fire.

For training purposes the 118th relieved companies of the 49th British Division, and the 118th's three battalions took over in rotation, each placing two companies in the front line in cooperation with the remaining British units. Each battalion occupied the forward area for eight days.

Lawrence and his fellow Americans found the front-line trenches at Ypres always a place to forget: the regular shellings, the sweeping of lines with machine-gun fire in predictable arcs, and at night the flares and the need for vigilance that made sleep almost impossible, resulting in grumpiness and tiredness by day. But one experience the South Carolinian would never forget: it consisted of accompanying an awkward American second lieutenant through no-man's-land and nearly getting shot. In the course of that affair the two men became lost, a very dangerous predicament in such a place.

I t is hard for me to remember the many impressions made upon my mind when I first took part in active warfare, but occasionally some little incident that impressed me comes back for a short time. Our entry into the line at Ypres was at night, under utmost secrecy, and we went up to our places quietly and cautiously in small units. The Germans were putting up flares that lighted no-man's-land and the trenches in spasmodic fashion, sometimes brightly, the flares dying down uncertainly, then suddenly a brightness that made it possible to discern any movement in no-man's-land. The flares made patrolling dangerous. They looked like the rockets used for Christmas fireworks, balls of fire trailed by streams of sparks. Because our position was a salient into German territory, it appeared as if the flares encircled us.

All of the men were a little nervous, which was natural because this was their first time under fire. There was a corporal in our company by name of Dewey Burch, from Cheraw, who took much pride in his squad. A young, impetuous fellow, he had managed to select his entire squad over a period of time, and endeavored to pick out large, ferocious-looking men. One day he pointed out one of his man-eaters and said, "Lawrence, there's a fellow that's going to give the Huns hell when he can get his hands on them." This fellow, named Bob

Bell, was a ferocious-looking fellow, tall and muscular, with the features of a fighter. In appearance he really did Dewey's squad credit. On the night we were going into the front-line trenches we halted for a short while in the shadow of a ruined building. Other American soldiers were there, among them Dewey Burch and his squad of desperate men. Shortly after we halted, Dewey came up to me and said,

"Come here, Lawrence. I want to show you something."

I followed, and much to my surprise saw the dangerous Bob Bell vomiting and shaking violently.

"What's the matter, Dewey?" I said. "Is he sick?"

"Naw," said Dewey, "the damn fool is scared to death."

"How are the other man-eaters?" I asked.

"Just about as bad," he replied disgustedly. "But the others are managing to hold their supper."

When at last we reported to the captain we were assigned to a section of the front-line trenches, and I was in command of my section, for which I had two squads—counting myself, seventeen men, a man for every yard of trench. We were cautioned to be alert, as the Germans opposing us were the best in their army. I arranged my men quietly on the fire step; each man stood and peered anxiously, a little nervously, into no-man's-land, ready to give the alarm at any sign of activity. We had to be careful how we looked over the trench's parapet, for the trench was built up with sandbags about three feet and the moon was shining behind us and silhouetted our line against the clear sky. At intervals German flares lighted the surrounding country brightly.

After an hour of standing-to the nervousness wore off, and I decided this was not so bad after all, so long as Jerry stayed in his own trenches. The thought of raiding

Jerry was not heartening. Lieutenant Brown came along and said we were to leave the trenches at midnight and crawl out beyond the wire and lie there until dawn, about 3:00 A.M. My orders were to deploy my men at wide intervals to watch for German patrols, and to keep the men from grouping. To my relief, I learned that the shift from the trenches to no-man's-land was both for vigilance and to clear the trenches before the Germans shelled them early in the morning.

My plan was that, together with the ranking corporal, Q. M. Davidson, I would go over first and find the gaps in the barbed wire, of which there were three separate entanglements running parallel with the trenches. The entanglements were about fifteen yards apart. The gaps for patrols to pass through were only about three feet wide and always covered by a machine gun in the trenches. After finding the gaps we were to guide the men through and deploy them beyond the last wire entanglement.

The experience of this first exploration into no-man's-land was, to say the least, enlightening. At midnight Q. M. and I took our positions in the trench opposite from where we thought the gaps were, waited until the flares died a little, then leaped to the parapet and over the top. I then had my first surprise, for I expected a drop of about three feet. As a matter of fact I fell headlong for six feet or more into a deep ditch. I lost my rifle and had to scratch around some time before finding it. Then I whistled softly for Q. M., who came crawling over; he had had the same experience. We stayed in the ditch some little time because of the flares, and watched our chance to begin crawling through the grass, which was about twelve inches high. I soon lost Q. M. in the darkness, and after crawling quite a way did not find the wire. Feeling quite alone, I crawled forward, sure the wire could not be far away. After covering quite a bit of ground by squirming through grass like a snake I decided I must have passed through all three gaps without seeing the wire, and this indeed is what had happened—I was quite a way into no-man's-land and in danger of blundering into a German patrol. Turning around I crawled back as far as I could and soon came to the wire, but neither Q. M. nor any of the men were anywhere to be seen. I started back to the trench and was overjoyed to find Q. M. at the second entanglement.

My adventure had a series of chapters, more or less. Not finding the men with Q. M., I told him to stay where he was and I'd go back and look for them, and after squirming back to the trench I found them, all fifteen of them, huddled in the bottom of the ditch into which I had fallen. Upbraiding them for not coming after us, I ordered them to crawl, one by one, to Davidson, who would direct them to their positions, and remained in the ditch until all had left. Following them I came to a shell hole and found five men huddled there, routed them out, and led them to their positions. Placing them, I found none of the others where they should be, and placed them one at a time.

All this activity attracted the Germans, who turned a machine gun on us. But for the depression in the ground in which we were lying we would all probably have been killed. Some of the men were in shell holes and pretty well protected, but half of them were out behind a little mound of earth. Part of my head was exposed, and several bullets hit within a few inches of my face. Dirt and rock struck my helmet, and several blades of grass were knocked in my face. Fortunately, not a man was hit.

I was much worried because I was sure the Germans had located us, especially so when the man next to me began vomiting and coughing. I thought he had been shot but found he was only scared. I sharply ordered him to keep quiet. Evidently he could not, because he started up again. I ordered him to crawl back to the trench, as he was endangering the whole detail. He was afraid to go alone, but I threatened him and finally got him started. He went about twenty yards and hid in a shell hole, where we found him on our way back to the trench.

After getting rid of him I looked at my watch, thinking we had been out there an hour or two, and according to the watch we had been out there fifteen minutes. It was the longest fifteen minutes I ever spent in my life.

The Germans fired on us as long as we stayed in no-man's-land, but not as furiously as at first. I suppose the only reason they did not try to capture us was because they suspected a trick; this same thing saved the Americans many times from the consequences of their blunders when first going into the line. After my men got into position they kept quiet with the exception of the man I chased back to the trench, and the Germans probably concluded that we had gone. But they traversed our whole line with machine-gun fire for the rest of the night—that is, a gun would start firing, rotate on its swivel, and thus distribute the fire along our trenches. They did this every night, and were so methodical that we could tell when to lie low, and after the fire passed over our heads we could ease up until it came along again at the regular interval.

Lying in no-man's-land that night I learned that a rifle or machine gun fired directly at one made a report much louder than if fired a little to one side. As the traversing machine-gun fire approached us the reports became louder, and when it passed overhead the reports were so loud it seemed the gun was no more than a few feet away. When I first experienced this illusion I thought we were being fired on at close range and every instant expected to see a German patrol leap toward us. I clutched my rifle with my finger on the trigger, bayonet fixed, thrust through the grass, ready to fire or lunge. Our resistance to any attack at this time would have been an individual affair, for we were so thinly spread out.

Fortunately that night the Germans confined their attack to strafing us with machine-gun fire, and after what happened to be an endless passage of time my watch showed 3:00 A.M. I gave the command to file back into the trenches, a command immediately obeyed. I followed last, with many an uneasy glance backward as I crawled along, dragging my rifle. Once back in the trench everyone felt better; the sick man got well, and the scared men got brave; they wanted to fire over the parapet to show their defiance. We stood-to until daylight, and after daybreak, with the exception of a few sentinels, retired to the shallow dugouts, ate breakfast, and slept through most of the day.

The next night we went through the same procedure, and I was gratified that the men were no longer nervous but took up positions in no-man's-land like veterans. Again the time hung heavy and Jerry traversed our lines with machine-gun fire, but we stayed out our time and returned to our trench without mishap.

The third night, lying in no-man's land, I heard someone approaching from behind. I pointed my rifle in the direction of the sound and waited until the figure approached, and it turned out to be our platoon officer, Lieutenant Brown—we called him "Mr. Hook" as he was awkward in his movements. He approached us with his bottom bobbing up out of the grass as if it was riding on wheels set off center, and said he wanted to inspect the wire entanglements and for me to get another man and go with him because he was unfamiliar with that section of the line. I selected a man and we started out, following the line of barbed wire nearest the German lines. Mr. Hook did not appear much interested in the wire and was more interested in the opposite direction, where he was casting anxious glances. We wandered on for several minutes, following him, and saw that he moved away from the wire while avoiding large shell craters. The first thing Mr. Hook and the rest of us knew, we were lost.

Being lost in no-man's-land was no joke. We crawled to where we thought the wire was and found no wire, and had to lie prone every minute or so to let the German traversing fire pass over us. This together with wandering around shell craters caused us to lose all sense of direction. We came to several pieces of wire entanglements, but they led us nowhere, proving to be isolated strands used before the present trench system was laid out. We crawled into a shell hole and admitted we were lost. I had a little compass with luminous figures, which we examined, and the needle pointed in the opposite direction from where we thought north should be; we were afraid to rely on the compass. Hook thought our lines were in a direction different from what I thought, and the other man had a different opinion. Finally we agreed to follow my direction, and crawled on hands and knees for a while, stopping every few seconds to listen, fearing we would blunder into a German patrol or the German trenches. We came to a barbed-wire entanglement, and in trying to crawl under it Mr. Hook got badly entangled. If the Germans had happened along they would have caught Mr. Hook like a rat in a trap. We did not know if this wire was ours or the Germans', and after rescuing Hook we followed it cautiously, lying flat on the ground or dropping in a shell hole every once in a while to escape the traversing fire. We kept this up, getting nowhere, and daylight was not far away and it seemed we were doomed to spend the day in a shell hole in no-man's-land; we could probably have located our trenches in daylight but could not expose ourselves to crawl to them. Suddenly a sharp "Halt!" rang out, in English, and English never sounded better. We quickly replied, "Friends." We had wandered into a group of our own men who were level-headed enough not to fire without a challenge.

We located our position from these men and crawled toward a gap in the wire they pointed out. When Mr. Hook reached the gap he stood up and rushed for the trench, and we followed, as big fools as he was. He reached the trench and tumbled in, and we followed and fell into the arms of several English soldiers who were swearing loudly. They bawled Mr. Hook out in good fashion. The corporal roared, "You bloody fools! You bloody fools! And you, an officer, to come through that gap and then rush at a trench like a bloody Jerry!" He upbraided Mr. Hook quite at length. "Didn't you know," he said to Hook, "that we had orders to fire on anyone coming through that gap? I had you all covered with my machine gun. I put my finger on the trigger three times to fire, but something stopped me. I thought about you bloody Americans. We took a chance of being butchered in our tracks by letting you come through!"

Mr. Hook did not have anything to say, but passed on down the trench without telling us goodbye or saying he had enjoyed the evening with us.

The English seemed to take the situation in these trenches more seriously than we did. Although we had charge of the trenches, English soldiers were left to man machine guns that covered the gaps in the wire entanglements. If it had not been for the carefulness of these three veteran English soldiers, we would have been riddled with their machine-gun bullets. I learned later that Lieutenant Brown had been told that this particular gap was dangerous and guarded carefully by the English.

The next day I walked around the traverse—that is, the corner—of a section of the trenches and bumped into an English soldier who, quick as a flash, thrust a pistol in my ribs. I jumped back and said, "What's the matter?" He did not reply, but grinned sheepishly, put his pistol back in the holster, and went back to his position on the fire step.

After returning from the "wire repairing" tour with Mr. Hook, I went back to the section of the trench held by my two squads and found they had returned from no-man's-land and were standing-to. After daylight we went to our dugouts and slept and loitered through the day, and explored the trenches in our vicinity, finding that our company was on the extreme left of the British line and joining the Belgians who held the line from that point to the sea. Three good-natured Englishmen acted as liaison between us and the "Belgiques," as they called the Belgians. I sat down on the fire step and chatted with them for a while.[1]

On the fourth night our company was relieved, and we retired three or four miles behind the front-line trenches toward Dirty Bucket, and three platoons were billeted in British defense trenches while the fourth was sent farther back to do detail work for the battalion. Mr. Hook, "Foots" Womack, and I occupied a small surface dugout in one of the trenches. Womack and I had found this little dugout, hardly large enough for the two of us, and had gotten all fixed when Mr. Hook happened along and decided he would move in. We managed to make room by lying on our sides. We could all just as well have slept on the ground in front of the trench, as it was perfectly safe. Mr. Hook seemed in good spirits and made several remarks to show how carefree he was, feeling probably that he was a veteran now that he had had several bad frights and was still alive. "If my mother only knew where I was tonight," he said, "she would be terribly worried." I thought that his mother never had any occasion to worry. Mr. Hook left us in a few days. Officers were needed back in the United States to teach recruits how to fight, so the captain sent Mr. Hook back as Company I's contribution.[2]

After a night and a day behind the lines we returned to the front line, and this time my platoon was in the third-line trenches, apparently a safe place but unfortunately not quite safe. The portion of trench occupied by the platoon crossed a paved street, which appeared to have been one of the main streets of Ypres. For dugouts we used the cellars of what had been stores. The third-line trenches were ordinarily safe from everything except shellfire, but ours occupied a dangerous position where it crossed the street, which ran into the German lines; from somewhere in their direction a machine gun played down this street. We never could find its position. If anyone exposed himself in the street in daytime the machine gun opened fire. One Englishman was killed, and one American wounded, in front of our cellar door. Once in the cellar we were safe. We spent the first night playing cards and relaxing. The cellar was sheltered enough for us to have a small candle.

On the second night, as I was preparing to spend a comfortable evening, our platoon sergeant, Hatfield, came in and gave me orders to report to Captain Gillespie with a squad of men to help put over a cloud gas attack. This probably was the last cloud gas attack launched by the Allies in the war, for gas shells thereafter replaced this method of using gas against the enemy.

We slung our rifles and filed out and reported to the captain, who told us that the British were preparing to put over the attack and that our job was to help them with the tubes and dig a passageway through the front-line trenches for a small cart to pass through. We found the cart, about as large as a pony cart, gathered up the necessary tools, and proceeded cautiously, led by the captain, from the third-line trenches toward the front line. Upon arrival, and getting to work, we dug slowly and quietly and were quite a while digging a gap wide enough. After we completed our job the English loaded the cart we brought with tubes, together with other carts, and hauled them into no-man's-land and placed them carefully, quietly in position. Gillespie in the meantime was stalking up and down in no-man's-land as if he had been walking down the streets of Cheraw.

The gas was not released until an hour before dawn, and as luck would have it the direction and velocity of the wind was perfect. The gas evidently was effective, as the Germans were greatly aroused and replied with a terrific artillery barrage, the worst I had seen up to that time. We were back in our third-line trenches about an hour before it began. Shells screeched toward us and exploded, throwing up clouds of earth. Fragments of shells whined over the top of our trench, and clods fell in on us from the parapet. We crouched close to the front side of the trench while the earth poured down on us. Every once in a while I peered over the parapet to see what was happening up ahead and thought the Germans probably were coming over. The men were unnerved, as this was their first heavy shelling. The big shells came screeching, louder as they got closer, and with a mighty rush exploding almost over us with a deafening roar, throwing dirt and debris in all directions. Before we could recover from one shell, another was repeating the punishment. Our line was badly battered, the dugouts caved in, some of our men partly buried. We had only four serious casualties, due principally to the well-constructed trenches. The shelling continued for about half an hour and died down.

It was shortly after the barrage that I came near being shot by one of my own men. After it seemed safe to stand up and look around I did so, and while looking things over saw a huge rat walking leisurely by, just behind the trench. I threw my bayonet at him but missed, and then jumped out of the trench and ran for the bayonet that had fallen about ten feet in the rear of the trench. As I turned back the nearest sentry, seeing me (it was not yet good daylight), quickly turned and fired point-blank. The bullet whizzed just over my head; he had fired before he brought his rifle to a level. My first thought was that he had seen a German about to attack me and was firing at him, and attempting to get under cover I made a leap for the trench in the direction of the sentry. As I landed in the trench he made a lunge at me with his bayonet, and I then realized he had taken me for a German. I closed with him and grasped his rifle and managed to calm him enough for him to realize what he was doing. Explaining the incident after he had calmed down, he said he saw me throw the bayonet and thought I was throwing a grenade at him, and when I ran toward the trench he felt sure I was a German. The fact was, he was unnerved from the shellfire and had completely lost his head. This man was a Swede named Sullivan, from Iowa, and he was later killed in action.

We withdrew from Ypres that night, never to return. All through the day Jerry showed a bad temper, thoroughly aroused over the gas attack. As darkness fell his temper worsened, and the heavy shelling set in again. Our relief was made under this shelling. The relief was the worst of our experiences in the Ypres sector, for as we attempted to file along the narrow paths, big shells exploded nearby and threw the men into confusion. The night was pitch-dark, and we had difficulty finding our way through the ruins of the town and over the trenches, through barbed wire, in and around shell craters. Sergeant Coward made a good guide and after many difficulties led us into a paved street that appeared clear of debris and with the walls of some buildings standing. Marching along, Coward suddenly stopped and said, "I do not believe I will go this way. It looks too good." His premonition saved our lives, because just as we turned up an alley we heard planes overhead that proved to be German, and they made themselves known by bombing the street; as the bombs struck the street they made the most deafening roar I had ever heard; the explosions were so loud and terrible they made us strangely weak. We felt helpless with those things dropping around us in the dark, with their frightful crashes and roars, and saw the few buildings left on the street blown to bits as the dark night was lighted for instants by the exploding bombs. We double-timed into another alley and onto the edge of the town, skirted what was left of the outskirts, and came to the bridge across the Ijser, where we found a scene of activity as shells were falling thick and fast. The supply company teams were waiting close by to carry back the heavy equipment and supplies, and their horses were rearing and plunging and the men swinging to the bits, swearing and cursing the details that had not come up with the things they were waiting for. We rushed across the bridge and struck out down the road at a fast pace, glad to leave Ypres behind.

★ IV ★
LANGRES

When General Pershing set up schools in France in the winter of 1917 and sent officers to them, the officers then returned to their units and instructed the men in what leaders of the AEF considered not merely the details of modern warfare that were worth the while of American troops but the proper doctrine by which the U.S. army would fight against the Germans when it at last entered the trenches. Pershing did not trust the training that officers and men received in the United States, believing it unrealistic. He felt that the War Department in faraway Washington did not understand modern war. Moreover, it had allowed British and French instructors to do much of the teaching. The leader of the AEF disliked instruction from the Allies, believing that Anglo-French ways were essentially defensive—unrealistic if the Allies, as he assumed, wanted to win the war. Only individual initiative, he stressed, could win on the battlefield, and this meant particularly the use of the rifle. When the ordinary soldier, trusting to his courage and ability in marksmanship, got out of a trench and engaged the enemy, the war could be won. Pershing's critics maintained that he ignored all the lessons of the Western Front, that he had no sense of the suicidal nature of individual actions by riflemen, that he was asking American soldiers to display the sort of spirit, the élan, *of British and French troops in 1914–15, before those troops realized the impossibility of winning the war through acts of individual courage. At AEF headquarters in Chaumont these protests were perceived as specious, almost as defeatist. No officer in the AEF dared champion trench warfare as anything other than a preparation for getting out of the trenches and moving forward to meet the enemy.*

During the winter of 1917–18 the officers schools disseminated AEF fighting doctrine to the troops, and yet to ensure that the U.S. army in France fought in the way Pershing desired it was necessary to continue the training of the most important—indeed the crucial— officers in the entire AEF, save perhaps field grade officers who planned strategy. The crucial officers in units were the second lieutenants, the men whose leadership ensured the carrying out of strategy. The AEF therefore sought out soldiers who had shown leader- ship and sent them to officers school at Langres, where after three months of training they became second lieutenants. Until the summer of 1918 the Langres school produced these "ninety-day wonders." By that time the front was consuming second lieutenants in large numbers, and Pershing shortened the course to sixty days. The latter was the requirement when Douglas Lawrence left his division in August to take the course at Langres.

W e had served our first hitch in the front line, been under heavy shellfire, patrolled no-man's-land, been bombed from the air, and suffered casualties. We felt like veterans. News had come of the victories by

American troops at Cantigny, Château-Thierry, and other places, and we knew it would not be long before we would take part in some big offensive. The first news I had of American participation in fighting was about a defeat of a unit of the 26th Division, told to me by British soldiers who shook their heads solemnly as if to say that they were afraid the Americans were not going to do much. We did not feel that way, wanted to get in the fight as soon as possible, and were certain we could hold our own.[1]

Upon leaving Ypres we journeyed—by narrow-gauge railroad and by marching—to a little town named Proven, still in Belgium. Proven and Watou were the only towns in Belgium within the Allied lines that had not been deserted by their inhabitants. Actually we were not in Proven but about two miles outside, in an army camp that had sufficient huts to shelter us all. The huts had earthen floors but were better than the outdoors. Here we spent the first day cleaning up and trying to rid our clothing of lice, known as cooties; I spent half a day picking these pests from my shirt, washed the shirt, and hung it up to dry in belief that I was rid of them, but next day I wore the shirt about an hour and began to feel the cooties in action again. I took my shirt off, found all of them had returned, and gave up in disgust. It was practically impossible to be rid of them, and the only successful way was to put clothes through a steaming process. They were a terrible nuisance, very uncomfortable, and I scratched so much my skin became sore.

The second day in Proven, several sergeants and I got passes and went into the town and enjoyed the leave. We ate at a good restaurant, went to a bathhouse and took a hot bath (the first in five weeks), and strolled around looking at the sights. Proven was a busy little city, and there was much activity, for soldiers of four nations—French, Belgians, British, Americans—were camped in the vicinity.[2]

I was at the Proven camp only two days when Captain Gillespie told me I had been selected to attend officers training school at Langres. I was one of twenty-five men selected from the regiment, and the only one from Company I. We were to start the next day.[3]

It was with regret that I told all my old friends goodbye, slung my pack, and walked toward the railroad station, never to see the 30th Division or any of its units again.

I found that our train was to leave not that night but the next morning, and we slept on the floor in the warehouse of the station. Next morning the train, consisting of those little freight cars built to hold eight horses or forty men, backed into the station. Forty-five of us got into a boxcar for an all-day and all-night ride.[4] Arriving at Rouen, and touring the town for a brief time, we marched across the town to another station. As usual, our heavy equipment bore down during the march, the hot sun made marching harder, and the paved streets added to the difficulty, and after about five miles we reached the station to find no train, for it was the wrong station. After two miles to another station it once more was, it seemed, the wrong station, but after much confusion we discovered that a train would come the next morning, so we marched to a French barracks for the night. After settling in there we again had a chance to see Rouen, very attractive, for the Seine flowed through the business district and on the side of the river the bank was lined with cafes with grassy lawns on which were tables and chairs for customers. The lawns were crowded with smart French civilians and French and British officers. Next morning we found our

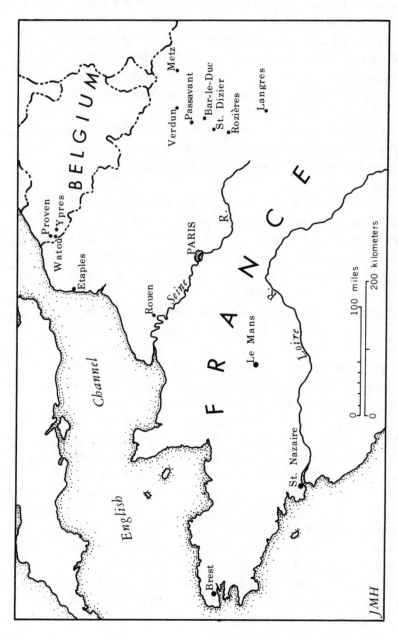

Southern Belgium, northwestern France, with Langres at bottom right

freight train, similar to the earlier one, and soon were heading along the banks of the Seine.

We arrived in Paris the following day at about 11:00 A.M. and marched into a building nearby where attractive French girls served us doughnuts and hot coffee, and then my South Carolina friend Fred Sexton, whom I had met after our train ride to Rouen, went with me to visit several cafes where Sexton took too many drinks, and did not want to return to the train.[5] Return we did, to discover to our delight that we were to leave Paris in third-class passenger cars instead of the little boxcars. We rode in a regularly scheduled train and were annoyed by passengers crowding into our coaches; we could not get rid of them as the train was moving, and several of them were women. At the next stop we refused to let more passengers into our car. We had a row with the train crew but easily disposed of them by shoving them out of the coach and threatening them with bayonets when they tried to reenter. That night I tried to get some rest by stretching out in the aisle, only to be awakened by an elderly Frenchwoman stepping on my legs; the train had stopped at a station and she had gotten on. She was hard to get rid of because we could not manhandle her, but we finally got rid of her before the train left the station by saying in our half-English, half-French: "American soldat partee pour le battlefield morte Bosche." The old lady replied, "Ah! Oui, oui, très bon," and left. Next morning, about 7:00, we arrived at the Langres station two miles from the city.

Langres is perched on a promontory-like mountain, almost a pinnacle, jutting from the tableland to which it is barely attached, out into the plains that spread on three sides as far as the eye can see. I do not know the elevation from the plains, but it must be at least four hundred feet—almost sheer. Once Langres was elaborately fortified with immense walls that rise from the edges of its precipitious limits. On the tableland side the walls fronted a deep moat. Surrounding country was dotted with underground forts. The Germans captured the city during the Franco-Prussian War but never threatened it during the World War. Langres in our time was a city of about twenty thousand inhabitants.

After the usual tortuous march we arrived at the officers training school known as Little West Point, and I entered the school with misgiving, having heard stories of the hard discipline and the difficulty in winning a commission. I had been told that candidates were watched every hour, day and night, in formation, in barracks, on leave in the city. This proved not altogether true, but almost. We were told that men made the best impression by being conspicuous. We knew the school rejected forty percent of the candidates. And so we marched into the quadrangle, so-called, a large open space almost enclosed by barracks and other buildings. We were divided into platoons and drew up in line in front of two barracks, and a slender, pale-faced, effeminate-looking second lieutenant took charge and addressed us in a snappy, girlish voice, said his name was Smith, explained what we had before us, and cautioned us about behavior. The more he talked the better I liked him, and when he finished I concluded we had drawn a good lieutenant; I learned later he was a Virginian.

Furniture in our barracks was double-decker bunks lining both sides of the long, narrow building, placed side by side with a space of three feet to the next group. Four men occupied each set of two. Fred Sexton and I took the two lower bunks in a set, and my South Carolina friend Clyde Singleton took a lower just opposite mine. After we took off our equipment and washed up we formed a mess line, received our food on the outside of a large stone building, and went into the building to eat at rough board tables. The meal was terrible.

Training now began in earnest. We met reveille at the usual time, ate breakfast, such as it was, and at the call of assembly formed our company in line of platoons and marched about a mile to a grassy field where each platoon went off by itself. Squads were arranged so as to obtain an alignment according to height, and I found myself near the short end of the line.[6] The day was devoted to close-order drill. Our training period lasted two months, August and September 1918, cut short a month because of the urgent need for officers at the front. Training was harsh and tried our endurance, patience, and pride to the limit. We did not have enough food, and what we had was bad; for ten days we existed altogether on bread and carrots—stewed carrots, carrot soup, carrot pie. Hours were from dawn till dusk, and at night we studied. On Saturdays we cleaned equipment and prepared for inspection. Once each week our platoon lined up on the field and the names of those deemed unqualified for commissions were read out; we were haunted all the time with fear that we would be sent back to our regiments. This procedure continued until our ranks had been reduced forty percent.

The training was thorough, including classroom instruction in tactics and strategy followed by exercises and maneuvers in the field. There was trench warfare, including construction, defense, raiding, scouting and intelligence, bayonet drill, gas war, machine guns, maps, use of airplanes and tanks and artillery. Open warfare was stressed because we were told that the war would not end until we drew the Germans into the open. Rumor reached us that the Americans were preparing a gigantic drive into thickly wooded and fortified country and our training would be cut short. The rumor was true; if the men who were working so hard for commissions could have seen ahead they would not have been so anxious to get them, for many were killed within two weeks after being commissioned.

The manner in which a candidate commanded a unit was an important factor in deciding whether he would make an officer, and there was a disagreeable tendency on the part of candidates not to work together. We thought that some men would be disqualified regardless of merit, and each man felt that if someone else was disqualified he himself would have a better chance; the result was that men in the ranks would not cooperate with the candidate in command of the company or platoon, and embarrassed him if they could. I was assigned to command the platoon in a complicated raid on a trench system and given responsibility for planning and directing the raid. Having in mind the poor cooperation received by candidates, I selected men for the principal parts whom I knew to be my friends, called them together, secured their help in planning, and stationed them in appropriate places. The rest of the platoon I distributed to inconspicuous places where they could do little. At the proper time I gave the signal and the raid got under way, with the officer-instructors looking on. It was a success and brought favorable comment. Each of my friends did his part admirably.

We were called before the major—a South Carolinian—on September 28, 1918, for examination, and waited in the hall outside while he examined us one by one. Wattie Anderson went in first and stayed quite a while, and when he came out we bombarded him with questions. He said the exam was severe and he was afraid he did not pass. We found later that he did. Humbolt Aull, of Anderson, was next; he stayed in twice

as long and came out downcast, and we learned later
that the major did not want to pass him but changed his
mind because of Aull's good record. Aull would
probably have been better off if he had not passed, for
shortly after he reached the front he was hit in the face
by a shell fragment and struck blind. Finally my time
came; I marched in, halted, saluted, the major stared
straight at me for a few moments, and then noticed the
regimental button on my collar—although not appropriate for my regiment at that time it said 2d South Carolina
Infantry, for it bore the letters "S.C." and the figure "2."
As mentioned, the major was from South Carolina.

"What part of South Carolina are you from?" said the
major.

"Florence, sir," I answered.

"That is all," said he.

My examination was over. I saluted and marched out.
Next day Lieutenant Smith assembled us in our barracks,
read the names of those to receive commissions, and my
name was on the list. With a few exceptions all the men
who survived the weeding out up to the time of the
examination were commissioned. The contingent from
my regiment, the 118th Infantry, formerly the 1st South
Carolina, made the best record of representatives of any
unit at the school. Of the twenty-five men sent from our
regiment, only one failed to be commissioned—this
when the average for the school was forty percent.

After we learned we were to be commissioned we
went into Langres to buy equipment, and Sexton and
Singleton and I went together. We first went to a bank
where I cashed a draft for $150 drawn on my account
with the State Bank of McBee. I lent $75 to Fred, and
then bought a Sam Browne belt, officer's knapsack,
raincoat, second lieutenant's bars, collar cross guns,
braid, and leather boots (the latter were to be the cause

of considerable suffering on my part, as they nearly ruined my feet). Next day we drew up in line and soon were dismissed, officers and gentlemen. We rushed to the barracks, donned our equipment, and roamed all over the neighborhood to try ourselves out on the enlisted men—we wanted to see if they would salute us. A few did, but most of them passed us by with only a disinterested glance.

Lieutenant Lawrence, after commissioning but before finding an officer's uniform

★ V ★
THE 29TH DIVISION

In the army nothing is predictable, procedures often are illogical, and so while it might have seemed sensible to assign Second Lieutenant Lawrence back to the 30th Division and even to the 118th Infantry, where he knew everyone, he was assigned to the 29th Division. He then had to find the 29th, no easy task. One might have thought that a unit as large as an American division would be easy to find, but divisions under Pershing moved frequently. Moreover, transportation was difficult into the battle areas in northeastern France, where the Germans had cut some of the railroads and traffic frequently passed along primitive roads. At last Lawrence found the 29th, but hardly had he met his platoon when the entire division was ordered up to the front.

T he day after we received our commissions at Langres, and after we stalked around among the enlisted men, our former comrades, to see if we could obtain salutes, we new officers received assignments and orders to join our new outfits. We formed in a single-file line and were assigned to combat divisions in groups of twelve officers. The first group went to the

First Division, and so on. My group was assigned the 29th Division, a National Guard division recruited from Virginia, Maryland, the District of Columbia, Delaware, and New Jersey, and known as the "Blue and Gray." We were almost assigned to our former division, the 30th; the only man from that division who was reassigned was named Grimes, an individual who later committed suicide because of brutal treatment from his colonel.

Our group, assigned to the 29th, marched off, and because Jack Blair was the first man standing in line in our group he was placed in charge of the detail. This was unfortunate, for Jack was a poor leader and wasted many hours because of lack of decision. His training in civil life had been clerical and legal, and he did not know how to handle men; otherwise he was a nice fellow. He was, incidentally, a hypnotist, and frequently put on a show for us in the barracks by hypnotizing some of the boys. He began by extending his arms straight in front of his body toward the face of his victim, staring straight into the man's eyes and repeating slowly, "You are asleep but don't know it." Soon he would have the man under his influence and doing all kinds of ludicrous things. Later, while we were trying to find the 29th Division under Jack's leadership, we many times became exasperated because of his inability to make up his mind and make a move. On such occasions we could taunt him by pointing our extended arms at his face and saying, "Jack, you are a damn fool and don't know it."

Our group consisted of Jack, Fred Sexton (Florence, S.C.), Clyde Singleton (Florence), John Wood (Ware Shoals, S.C.), Robert M. ("Uncle Bun") Bailey (Anderson. S.C.), E. L. McCants (Anderson), Wattie Anderson (Easley, S.C.), D. M. Lyons (hometown unknown), Tilmer A. Running (some northwestern state), F. Mims (Fort Mill, S.C.), Harry A. Johnson (Fayetteville, N.C.), and myself. We marched out of the barracks late in the afternoon of October 1, 1918, through the streets of Langres, down the steep hill to the station where we were assigned compartments in a passenger train, which pulled out in about an hour and we were on our way, we knew not where—other than to join the 29th Division.

Late in the night we were awakened from our dozing by the rumble of artillery fire, and could see a glow from the flashes of the guns in the distance; we were approaching the front. After daybreak we stopped at a small village and alongside was a large barbed-wire enclosure filled with German prisoners who were guarded by about ten black soldiers. We called to the guard closest to us and said, "Where did you get all those Jerries?" He replied with a grin, "We cotched 'em las' night."

After the train left the village it seemed to be going away from the front, for the sound of firing began to die away, and this proved the case, because at about ten that morning we arrived at St. Dizier, a sizable town a safe distance beyond the German guns. Having arrived, however, we did not know what to do, and Jack consulted his papers and after study decided that the instructions were too vague. Clyde Singleton deserted to hunt for something to eat, and I wanted to go but felt we should stay together. Upon inquiry we found a Franco-American so-called rest camp where we managed a poor breakfast. Here we found we could leave St. Dizier that night by train for a railhead and base hospital that was on our way. We spent the day loafing about town, exposing ourselves to enlisted men for salutes.

After entraining that night and arriving at the railhead and base hospital before daybreak, about seventy-five miles on our way to the front, we again could hear the big guns and see the ambulances coming directly from the battlefield. Here our first concern was food, and Clyde located a kitchen and arranged things, as he had been a mess sergeant. We accidentally met a detail of sergeants from the 29th Division en route to Langres, and these men gave us the first accurate information we had about where the 29th Division was—it was at Verdun.

Again it was a train ride, this time an ammunition train that left for the front at night. We were assigned a boxcar partly loaded with what seemed to be cast-iron pipes and gun-carriage parts. But after about ten miles the train stopped, and we were advised to get out and walk. We had stopped close to the Verdun highway, and soon were on our way, hiking toward the city. Traffic was heavy, mostly trucks and ambulances, and we met units of the 42d (Rainbow) Division coming from the front.[1] They looked as if they had had a hard siege of it. I was attracted by the youthful looks of a captain of a machine-gun company, who looked to be about twenty-one or twenty-two. We had trouble finding food this day and had to depend on what we could buy from the few French peasants who had not retreated before the enemy. After a long day's hike we at last decided to spend the night in a barn on the roadside, where we found enough hay for our beds.

The trip seemed to go on interminably. We were up early in the morning and off without breakfast, and as we hiked along the troops became more numerous. Signs of shellfire appeared—shell craters, destroyed buildings. About nine that morning we came to a partly destroyed village occupied by part of the American Fifth Division, resting in this back area. They had been in the line and not performed well. We managed to get breakfast from one of their kitchens.

Here we had a disagreement as to how to proceed, for we had tired of hiking and thought that Jack should arrange with the Fifth Division for transport. Jack disagreed, so Singleton, Anderson, and Lyons deserted the detail in disgust. I never saw Singleton and Lyons again until after we returned from the Argonne, and I never saw Anderson thereafter. The rest of us headed down the Verdun highway and early in the afternoon arrived at the outskirts of the city or what the Germans had left of it. After being misdirected into the city, to a fort, and failing to find the 29th Division headquarters, though getting a good view of the bloody battleground where the French had stopped the German attack toward Paris, we met two French officers who shrugged and grunted about the location of the division, and again Jack could not decide what to do. Fred Sexton and I started toward Verdun again, alone, and the others followed. We reached the main part of the town, where we found a battery of coast artillery preparing a meal, and we persuaded them to include us in the party. We then were in better spirits and soon found 29th Division headquarters in the citadel of Verdun, a part of the fortifications of the city. Blair went in and reported and came out with instructions to report to the headquarters of the 57th Brigade and with information as to how to find it, a frame building in a patch of woods several miles from the town. Again Blair went in and reported, and while we were waiting Major General Morton, the division commander, walked out. We all saluted, and he acknowledged the salute.[2]

Blair returned with our assignments. Bailey and Running were assigned to the 114th Infantry, and were

General John J. Pershing and Major General Charles G. Morton

both killed in action within a few days. Blair, Sexton, Wood, McCants, Mims, and I were assigned to the 113th, which we found to be a New Jersey regiment. Of the detail that left Langres, seven got into the Argonne battle, and of those men three were killed, two seriously wounded, and two escaped without serious injury. The last two were McCants and I.

Receiving our assignments we proceeded to our regiments, and it was raining and we plodded down the shell-torn road, went through the little town of Nixeville, badly scarred by the war and swarming with American and French soldiers, and just outside on a thickly wooded hill named Moulin Brule, just about dusk on Sunday, October 6, we found the 113th Infantry encamped in wooden barracks. The commander, Colonel William R. Pope, a Regular Army officer, shook hands with us and said, "I am glad to see you gentlemen. We need you badly." He assigned us to companies— Blair to Headquarters, John Wood to B, McCants to G, Mims and me to L, Sexton to M. Sexton and I were disappointed not to be assigned to the same company, for we had been together since we met on our way to Langres.

Mims and I reported to Lieutenant Charles Grassey, in command of Company L, a short, stocky man with a large nose dominating a "hard-boiled" face. It was dark when we found him in the little hut he and several officers were occupying, and he peered at us in the dim candlelight and said, after we had reported, "Are you guys officers?" As if to say that we did not look the part. We said we were. I said I was a native of Virginia, enlisted in South Carolina. His next remark was, "My God, another Virginian. I have two and don't want any more. You Virginia birds don't hate yourselves, do you?" I decided I was not going to like Lieutenant Grassey. He then searched around and found bunks for us and introduced us to the other officers, and I met Second Lieutenant Derrickson, who advised me, when Grassey was out of hearing, that the lieutenant was a bum and not being a gentleman did not know how to treat one. Derrickson was a Virginian, from Norfolk, and had worked with my brother Lewis, it turned out. Grassey was from Paterson, New Jersey.

After we had our bunks and disposed of our equipment Grassey took us to the kitchen and introduced us to Mess Sergeant Si Marsicano, a tall, powerful man with a pleasant, friendly manner. Grassey told us that Si accidentally had shot First Sergeant Murphy in the leg with a .45 automatic the day before.

While we were eating, Grassey told us the regiment had expected to move up to the front that night but just before we arrived had received orders to remain at Moulin Brule. He assigned Mims to the second platoon and me to the third. After we finished, Grassey had our platoons assemble so he could present us to the men. There still was likelihood we would move to the front before daybreak.

Here, then, I met my platoon.[3] Grassey introduced me to Platoon Sergeant E. A. Mattson and thereupon left. I spoke a few words to the men and dismissed them. The other two sergeants, A. L. Meier and G. A. Janz, came up and introduced themselves. Mattson was from New Jersey, and Meier was a native-born Swiss and from Jersey City; Janz, with an officer uncle in the German army, was from Hoboken. I discovered later that Meier was the most dependable man among the three, though he had a weakness for drink; he was about forty years old, short and stocky, curt and abrupt. Mattson was slight in stature, tow-headed, talkative, and flighty. Janz was young, well built, and weighed about 160 pounds.

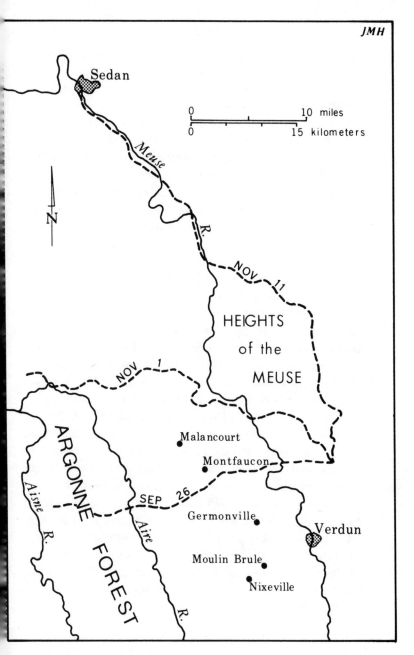

Battle of the Meuse-Argonne, September 26-November 11, 1918

After talking to the sergeants for a few minutes I returned to the barracks and went to bed.

At the time I joined the 29th Division it was in reserve for the Meuse-Argonne battle, an area where after severe fighting and heavy losses the American army had made substantial advances but in so doing had exposed its right flank to enfilading artillery and machine-gun fire from the fortified heights of the Meuse on the east side of the river just across from the exposed right flank. The German fire from this quarter was so severe that the right of the American line could not advance. The heights of the Meuse had to be cleared, regardless of the cost, and this task was assigned to the 18th (French) Division and the American 29th and 33d. The Germans were expecting an attack on the east bank, as shown in a captured order: "It is certain that the Franco-Americans are going to attack east of the Meuse on a great scale. We have not been able to determine whether the attack will extend to the left bank. The situation demands the greatest surveillance. Under no circumstances is the enemy to be able to surprise us."

After joining the 113th at Moulin Brule woods I spent a day in an effort to find equipment for myself, and Mims and I went with Grassey to the supply tent in search of pistols, but the best that the supply officer, Captain Newell, could do was to issue us pistol holsters. Grassey therefore borrowed a .45 automatic for each of us from the enlisted men. I still lacked a compass, field glasses, trench knife, mess kit, overcoat, and blanket, especially the last two items, and suffered for lack of them because of the cold, rainy weather, until I salvaged them on the battlefield, and eventually salvaged all the other equipment.

★ VI ★

TO THE HEIGHTS OF THE MEUSE

The Battle of the Meuse-Argonne, the greatest American engagement of the war, in which 1.2 million men took part, nearly 100,000 were wounded, and 26,000 were killed, opened September 26, 1918, and continued until the Armistice on November 11. The terrain was extremely difficult, and when the Allied commander-in-chief, Marshal Ferdinand Foch, gave the Meuse-Argonne to the Americans he may have thought they would accomplish nothing in that awful place with its thick woods and open areas ringed by German artillery on the heights to the east of the Meuse River, north of Verdun, and in the Argonne Forest to the left. Pershing had insisted on an American field army, rather than brigading his troops with the British and French, and was highly critical of Allied strategy and tactics. He had no experience of war beyond the Spanish-American War, in which he was a major of volunteers, and the Filipino Insurrection in which he was a captain. At the end of the Moro campaign President Theodore Roosevelt promoted him from captain to brigadier general. During the Mexican border expedition of 1916 he had pursued Pancho Villa without result and became a major general. Foch may have believed that the Meuse-Argonne was the place for him. The battle

*called on all the American commander's steely
resolution. He opened the Meuse-Argonne with untested
divisions, because of the too brief period after an
operation at St. Mihiel in which his troops wiped out a
German salient in four days, September 12–15; it was
difficult to shift 300,000 men sixty miles from one
front to the other under cover of night marches. Initial
fighting went well and troops gained the heights at
Montfaucon. Then the battle reduced itself to frontal
assaults through wild terrain, up one ravine, down
another, German troops disputing every foot. It was at
this juncture that Pershing discovered his forces were
being enfiladed by fire from the heights of the Meuse
and dispatched two divisions, one of them the 29th, to
seize the heights.*

*Taking the Meuse heights was bound to be difficult.
As American troops looked toward the river they could
see the long marshy valley—open ground without
cover. Along the Meuse, running north-south, lay the
highway to Verdun, the only sizable road, on which
German artillery was certain to have zeroed in. Two or
three miles on the other side rose the large forests—
Consenvoye, Ormont, Haumont—in which the Germans had placed their artillery. The 29th Division was
to attack with its 58th Brigade, the 116th Infantry on
the right, the 115th on the left. The 57th Brigade
(113th, 114th) was held in reserve. To the division's left
would be the 33d Division, to its right the French 18th.
The entire force was under the French XVII Corps. The
Germans had spent two years, since the Battle of
Verdun, fortifying the heights. The division was going
to have to fight its way through heavily wooded ridges,
steep-sided ravines, and large farms with cleared fields.
Automatic weapons, with which the defenders were
well supplied, could sweep those fields. Many German*

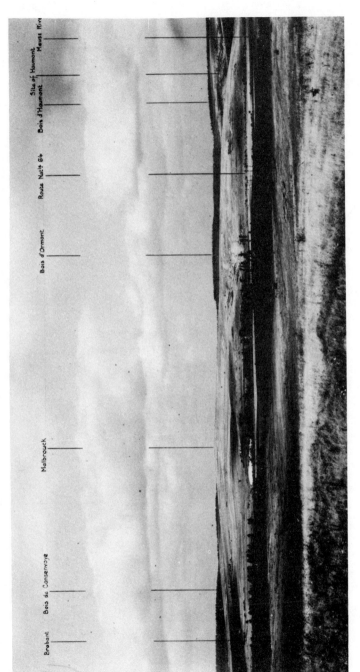

The heights of the Meuse

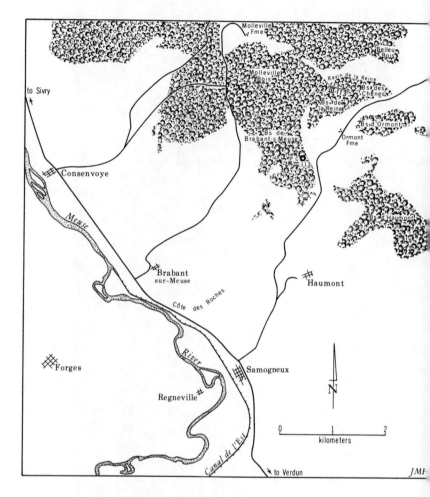

The heights of the Meuse

machine-gun nests were built of concrete, immune to artillery fire short of a direct hit. A system of narrow-gauge railroad tracks allowed the defenders to bring up heavy loads of supplies and ammunition—whereas the attacking Americans had left their railheads far behind.[1]

During the first day of the attack on the Meuse heights, October 8, 1918, the result for the Allies was not altogether satisfactory, and it was for that reason that my regiment, the 113th, was called in. The plan of attack on October 8 was for an assault by the 18th French Division and the 58th Brigade of the 29th Division. The brigade consisted of the 115th (Maryland) Infantry and the 116th (Virginia) Infantry. The attack was preceded by heavy artillery fire from the 158th Artillery Brigade (American), and at 5:00 A.M. the infantry attacked vigorously, the Maryland regiment advancing rapidly as the 1st Austro-Hungarian Division gave way. The Virginia regiment met resistance from the 15th German Division and did not reach its objective until the second day of severe fighting. The French met so much resistance that they advanced little and were far short of their objective on October 9, the second day. By that time the Austro-Hungarians had been replaced by veteran Germans.[2]

When the attack did not reach all its objectives on the initial day, October 8, we learned that our regiment was to move into the line that night, and Mims and I had supper with a group of French and American officers and speculated on what the night and morrow would bring.

"Our boys are in good shape," Lieutenant Derrickson said, "and are going to push hard when they meet the Germans tomorrow."

In my mind I reviewed what I would do when we made the assault, for although I had been in action I never had taken part in an attack on a fortified position. I thought of mother, members of my family, my sweetheart, but had no premonitions, though I would have been glad for the war to have ended that night. A French officer sitting next to me at the table poured cognac in my coffee, which nearly made me drunk, and I was unsteady when I got up from the table and for some time thereafter.

About 9:00 P.M. the command was given to "fall in," and it was the darkest night I think I ever saw, cold and raining, and the camp was a sea of mud. Our company formed in the barracks, and I took my position at the head of my platoon, the command was given, and we marched in column of twos out of the barracks and into the inky blackness. I could not see the man ahead of me, and had to reach out and grasp his coat, and the man behind me did likewise, and in this manner we struggled through the woods and down a long hill to the highway where, out of the woods, we could see a little better. Here we formed in column of squads and began a march filled with hardship and suffering—for I think that the long march from the Moulin Brule woods to the Meuse River was more severe and trying than the long, cruel march in July from northern France into Belgium.

The highway was in bad condition, having been cut up by the heavy army traffic and by shellfire, and it was difficult to keep the men in formation, for there also was the rain and the darkness. A man would slip off into the deep ditch by the road, and his comrades would drag him back, wetter, muddier, in decidedly a worse frame of mind. It was so dark I could not tell if a man was in danger until I heard him splash. The column became ragged, and Grassey ordered me to the rear to keep the men from straggling. It was not easy to keep the men in order, for they were wet to the skin, their equipment heavy, with every step they had to drag their feet out of the sucking mud. I met some resistance until Sergeant Meier came to my assistance, and after a while we somewhat improved the column.

At last, after two hours, dark outlines of buildings appeared, and we found a village with the peculiar name of "Germantown."[3] We were so tired we thought we would halt there and billet for the night, but no such luck; we found later that we had just gotten started. Still, the roads were better, and the column swung through Germantown at a brisk pace, into the hills beyond. We halted near the top of a high hill and stood and shivered in the cold rain for about half an hour before being given the command to fall out, after which we were not much better off because there was no place to sit down except on the muddy road or the wet ditch banks. Many of the men lay down in the mud or on the ditch bank and went to sleep. I sat on the bank and gazed at the endless glow from the gun flashes as the Franco-American and Austro-German artillery roared at each other. I tried to go to sleep but could not, for I did not have an overcoat or blanket and was so chilled I could not doze; my light raincoat offered little protection against the rain, none against the cold. After about two hours the word passed along to fall in, and the column moved forward. I was glad, because the marching warmed me. We were told from one source that the halt was caused by the Germans' shelling of the road ahead and from another source that the guide lost his way. I was inclined to believe the latter, for we did not hear any exploding shells ahead.

After several more hours of marching we turned off the road into a thick woods and halted for the rest of the night, but orders were given not to unroll blankets as we might have to move into the line on a moment's notice. Smoking was prohibited and all lights banned. I lay there in the cold, drizzling rain until my feet and hands became numb, and got up and walked around so as to get warm, and discovered a horse tethered to a tree, covered with a nice warm blanket. I thought I would borrow the blanket for a while, so unbuckled the straps and took it off. The poor horse began to shiver and whine, so I put it back on him and lay down on the wet ground without a blanket until dawn. We were in range of the German guns and an occasional shell exploded nearby, but we had no casualties; we were told that a shell fell in a group of men camped there the day before and killed and wounded several of them. Shortly after daybreak we had a breakfast of cold coffee and bread, and it had stopped raining but still was cold.

We resumed the march on the morning of October 9. The road was jammed with traffic. As we marched from the woods into the road we met a long French column coming from the front and saw an American artillery regiment on the road going in the same direction as ourselves. The three columns had to share the road. We were on one side, the French going in the opposite direction in the middle. We managed to get along until we met some French horse-drawn caissons, and one driver drove his team into my platoon, forcing some of my men into the ditch, so I grabbed the bridle of the nearest horse and jerked him into the ditch. One wheel of the caisson ran off the road into the ditch, throwing the driver, who swore in French and I replied in English.

As far as we could see, on all sides we were in an area of great activity, for the American army was engaged in its greatest battle just ahead. The area behind the fighting lines was a beehive; ammunition was moving up, supply trucks, ambulances were bringing back the wounded, exhausted troops were plodding toward the back areas, and here and there were batteries of artillery in position, barking viciously at the Germans, with airplanes overhead, military police everywhere, and fresh troops like ourselves moving into the line. A few days before, the area through which we were marching had been the battlefield. The Austro-Germans had fallen back but were putting up a stubborn resistance.

About noon we turned from the road into a meadow, halted, and broke ranks. The ground underfoot was so wet we could not sit down, and we could do nothing but stamp around in the mire. The skies overhead were dark, and it looked like more rain. On a hill behind were several batteries of American artillery, firing rapidly and steadily. Toward the lines, about two miles ahead, was a long hill over which German shells were bursting. For a distance along the skyline the shells appeared to be just clearing the summit and bursting on our side, but they were at least two miles short of us. It was fascinating to watch them and to see the American batteries behind us vigorously in action.

When the time came for the midday meal we received the disturbing news that the Company L kitchen had fallen into a ditch and spilled our dinner in the water, but Company K divided its meal with us, such as it was— stewed corn and tomatoes, beans, and coffee. It started to rain hard about the time I got my mess kit filled, and the water so diluted my food and coffee that I had about ten percent food and ninety percent rainwater.

My feet were paining me, for the new boots made large blisters, which had burst. The water had of course soaked through, and my feet were wet. But I spent most of the time in the meadow getting acquainted with my men, talking with them.

About 8:00 P.M. the command was given to fall in, and in column of twos we again headed into the darkness, this time for the front line. We were in support of the 58th Brigade (115th and 116th Infantry), hotly engaged with the Austro-Germans. The lot of a support unit, it turned out, was not an easy one, for we were only a few miles behind the fighting line, moving forward as the Americans advanced and stopping as the advance slowed, harassed by the German shells that fell all around us, and ready to go into the line on a moment's notice.

We marched toward the fighting lines on what had been a railroad fill. Shellfire had destroyed the railroad and dug great craters and gaps in the fill, and we could not see them in the darkness and did not find them until one or more men would fall headlong. I walked into one and fell several yards head over heels, and had difficulty finding my platoon when I dragged myself out. We came to what had been a village on the banks of the Meuse, now only a mass of broken bricks and stone, and stumbled over the debris with difficulty, attempting at one place to go through a narrow passage about three feet wide between two walls. At the same time a French stretcher detail tried to pass, carrying several wounded soldiers, and there was confusion, our men and the stretcher bearers jostling each other and swearing, the wounded crying out in pain; it was so dark we did not know we had collided with a detail of wounded until we heard the cries and groans. Shelling was heavy, exploding all around in rapid succession, and the French were anxious to get away with the wounded; I had a glimpse of a wounded French officer as I was jostled by his stretcher bearers.

We passed down a steep hill to the Meuse and crossed rapidly on a pontoon bridge; not a minute too soon, for just as the last man was safely across a shell struck the bridge in the middle, blowing it to bits.

We struggled through the darkness on a congested road parallel to the river, turned to the left up a short incline, and found ourselves later (we could not see at the time) in a valley between two bald hills. As we turned from the road into the valley we were guided through a gap in the barbed-wire entanglements by our YMCA man, "Centîmes," and that was the last I saw of him or any other auxiliary serviceman on the front, for it was no place for noncombatants.[4] Passing through the wire entanglement I fell and scratched my hands badly on the barbed wire. The whole regiment marched into this valley, called the Côte des Roches, and broke ranks, again with strict orders not to unroll blankets or make lights of any kind. We were to be prepared to make an attack any hour, to "move in" on a moment's notice.

It was a miserable lot of men who sat around in the darkness on the ground in the cold rain, under enemy shellfire, waiting for conditions still worse—an attack on veteran troops, fortified, a foe at bay. The men were in good spirits, though there was the usual grumbling; they would not have been soldiers if they had not grumbled. After we broke ranks and groped around for resting places we found the valley was pitted with large shell holes. The craters afforded protection from the weather and shellfire, but they had been occupied before and in most cases were filthy. Still, they were better than the open ground. Looking for a likely hole to spend the few remaining hours of night I found a large one, about the size of an ordinary room in a house, occupied by five or six of my men. I slid in, and upon getting closer to them found they had ignored orders and unrolled their blankets. I asked if they did not know they were disobeying orders, and they replied that they were so cold and tired they decided to take a chance. I told one of them, named Mason, to move over and I would share his blanket, but soon found I had selected a bad one, for just as I got comfortable a shell exploded and threw Mason into a panic, and he jumped up, scrambled out of the hole, and fled into the darkness with "our" blanket clinging to him. Finally he found his way back. I scolded him—he was only a boy—for lack of nerve, and he promised it would not happen again; but it happened three or four more times. I gave up and joined two men who had their blankets unrolled, was soon asleep in spite of the shelling, for the first time in forty-six hours, and slept a full hour.

At three in the morning of October 10 we received an order to attack a German position where the French had been repulsed. We were but a few minutes forming column and on our way to go "over the top."

We marched briskly in the chilly morning air, out of the valley of the Côte des Roches, into the shell-torn highway that ran along the Meuse, where we met long columns of tired artillerymen, relieved from the front, plodding toward the rear, guns drawn by wretched horses suffering from the poison gas that polluted the air all along the front. Ambulances rocked over the rough road with their burdens of suffering humanity, the suffering made worse because of the jostling. Details of prisoners were being herded to the rear by military police. Shortly after our column straightened out in the highway the shelling became severe, and big shells fell in the river a few yards to our right and along the hill nearby on our left, with deafening crashes, throwing mud and water and fragments right and left, high into the air. The fire was directed along the highway, for the Germans knew it was under constant use. Our men were jittery, for shellfire has a demoralizing effect; soldiers do not mind bullets but screaming, screeching, exploding shells twist and tear at their nervous systems; even veterans jerk and twist when lying inactive under a heavy barrage. A large shell screamed a few feet over the heads of my men, and they fell to their knees as if they were one man, throwing the column into disorder. I rallied them back into position in the moving column.

We turned left and headed into the line of combat, which appeared to be about a mile or two ahead, judging from the rifle and machine-gun fire. We were passing over the scene of the struggle the day before, between the 116th Infantry and the Germans, and it was daylight and we could see signs of the struggle, for all the dead had not been buried; I stepped aside to avoid stepping in a bloody mess of flesh and scraps of an American uniform—evidently the unfortunate fellow had been hit by a shell. Pieces of a rifle lay nearby. A little farther we crossed a trench demolished by shellfire, and I saw three dead men lying on the bottom as if the three had died in combat; two were Americans and one a German, and the German lay on his back with his chalky-ink swollen face hideous in death; one American lay crumpled on his face, the other in a half-sitting position with legs apart, knees bent upward, arms thrust forward, as if warding off his assailant. I could almost reenact the struggle that took three lives. We marched up a hill and halted near the top, where it developed later that our battalion commander, Captain Winterton, had lost his way. While we waited for him to find it, tear gas shells began to fall, and we put on our masks and the battalion retired down the hill. We retraced our steps a few hundred yards and continued up the valley into which we had turned from the highway. We passed through what was known as Ormont Farm and into a thick woods where the rifle and machine-gun fire appeared to be only a hundred yards away. In fact we were within a hundred or a hundred and fifty yards of the front line. The trench line was up ahead, out of sight, on the edge of the woods away from us. Companies K and M moved forward and occupied the trenches as the French troops moved out by the right flank. Our Company L, together with Company I, remained in the rear of the trenches in a sheltered position in the woods, by a stream in a narrow valley between two steep-sided hills. A machine-gun unit occupied the crest of the hill to our left and was firing noisily on the German lines ahead. As we advanced from the highway up the valley toward the front we left the shellfire behind us, but I knew we soon would have more when the Germans got the range of the machine guns on the hill.

Close by where we were resting, waiting to attack, was a group of perhaps six German officers' graves, enclosed by a picket fence, marked with neatly carved wooden crosses with the officers' spiked helmets fastened to the crosses. When I passed that spot some days later I noticed that the graves had been stripped of the crosses and helmets.

★ VII ★
INTO THE WOODS

Lawrence and his men attacked into the woods, and soon the fight was everywhere and, it appeared, almost without order. On the larger scene was far more order than Lawrence imagined, for with few exceptions no units of the regiment were lost; officers knew what was going on. But the work of war was on the local level, in the woods with Lawrence's platoon of Company L.

The order of attack of the 113th Infantry on October 10, 1918, was the 3d Battalion (ours) in the assault, 2d Battalion in support, and 1st Battalion in reserve. Order in our battalion was Companies K and M in the assault, Companies I and L (ours) in support, with L supporting K.

As zero hour, 11:00 A.M., approached and we formed in line to occupy the trenches when Companies K and M left them, my men began discarding their packs in spite of the general order that all troops must have packs on when going into battle. The men would need their blankets and other equipment, and the packs afforded protection against shell fragments. I ordered the men to put their packs back on, and several replied that they did not want to be weighted down with packs strapped to their backs when they encountered Germans. I half agreed, and before I could insist on the packs we were ordered forward as Companies K and M left the trenches and, with the French on their right, were rushing, under cover of our artillery and machine-gun barrage, toward the German lines.[1]

The big assault on the Germans was under way, the 113th Infantry under Colonel Pope making the attack, supported by the 111th Machine Gun Battalion commanded by Major Millard Tydings (later senator from Maryland) our battalion forming the spearhead.[2] Our two companies, L and I, occupied the vacated trenches just long enough for the attacking companies to get the proper distance.

The assaulting line met a withering machine-gun and rifle fire, for the Germans had a concealed trench about one hundred and fifty yards in front of Company M. A heavy enfilading fire came from Ormont Woods on the right. Casualties were heavy; the first assault line was mowed down, Lieutenant Trestrail commanding Company M was killed, Lieutenant Webb badly wounded, and my friend Fred Sexton was next in command.[3] The line staggered but managed to push slowly forward. Then the French on the right staggered, broke, and went back, leaving our right-flank Company M "in the air." Company K was also having trouble, for the line of advance was up a long, steep slope, open for the most part, dotted with two or three small patches of woods. Company K, struggling forward under heavy fire, suffered many casualties and obliqued to the right, leaving a dangerous gap between their left and the position of the 116th Infantry. Now both flanks of the battalion were in the air, and Company I was thrown in to extend the line to the right and protect that flank, and we—Company L—were thrown in to extend the line to

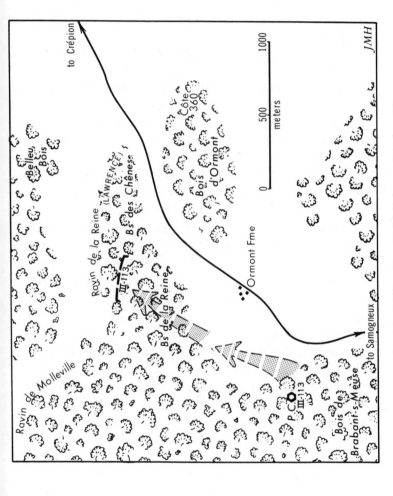

Line of attack, 3d Battalion, 113th Infantry, October 10

the left, fill the gap, and assault the Germans in that sector. Because of the failure of the French, two companies from the 1st Battalion in reserve moved up to protect our right flank.

When we occupied the trenches momentarily I inspected my platoon in haste and found everything in order except that most of the men had discarded their packs. They appeared in good spirits in spite of their perilous position. We were in the trench only a few minutes when the events described above occurred and Grassey called the officers together—Mims, Derrickson, and me—and said we were to go over immediately. He explained our line of advance, after which we returned to our positions. He then gave the signal, I leaped to the trench parapet, followed by my men, formed them in line of combat groups (squads in single file), and quickly deployed them, for the fire was so heavy. Lieutenant Grassey, the man whom I had so disliked upon first encounter, handled the company well; he was cool, collected, and directed our advance with skill.

We went forward by rushing a few paces and falling in shell holes, if available. If not available, we fell flat on the ground. While we were advancing the German artillery opened on us for the first time since the assault began, and this made matters worse, for the shells fell thick and fast, coming toward us screaming and screeching, louder and louder, striking the ground in front or behind with a deafening, demoralizing crash, hurling dirt and debris all over us. It was remarkable we were not killed; I saw a shell hit between two of my men who were not over four feet apart, and they were covered with dirt and badly shocked but otherwise unhurt. I had difficulty keeping my line straight and moving forward in the midst of this chaos, and the men gathered in groups in spite of all the sergeants and I could do, but we did fairly well. Resistance was so determined that the other companies stopped about halfway up the slope. My platoon was pressing forward when I received word from Grassey to halt where I was because the other companies were held up and could not advance. Sergeant Mattson and I occupied a shell hole, and the other men crawled into shell holes. About fifty yards ahead of us was a small patch of woods, and I observed that when we advanced from our present position, if we could, about half my line would be in the woods and the other half still in the open; I planned to get as many men into the woods as I could.

I do not know how long we stayed in our position waiting for units on our right to advance, for it seemed like hours. An attempt was made to break the German lines with machine guns, and as I lay in my hole I saw the machine gunners rush forward through the infantry and mount their guns. I do not believe they fired a shot; the gunners were mowed down before they could pull a trigger. Those that could, dragged themselves into shell holes and abandoned their guns. Our colonel was later criticized by General Morton for the loss of life caused by using the machine gunners out of place in an assault of this kind, for he contended that if the infantry could not break the enemy lines, machine gunners who were handicapped with heavy equipment and guns that could be mounted only in exposed positions should not be expected to do so.[4]

It seemed several hours before we attempted to advance again, and we kept up a rifle duel with the Germans in the trench ahead while their artillery blasted our lines. We were attacked from the air by a plane firing on us with a machine gun.[5] It would appear that we all should have been killed under the heavy fire, but men properly placed in shell holes make poor targets for all weapons except grenades, and we were too far from the Germans for them to use grenades effectively. Our battalion nonetheless suffered many casualties. My platoon probably was the most fortunate one in the battalion, because up to this time I had not lost a man; we had many miraculous escapes.

I was short one man, who deserted when we went over the top. The first sergeant of our company also deserted, with several other men of the company. There always were desertions when an outfit went over, and I estimated later that they amounted to an average of four or five to a company for every major assault. Many men cannot muster the courage to jump from a trench and rush the enemy in the open, whether they wear an American uniform or not. Our first sergeant, Murphy, gave me his field glasses a little while before we jumped off, saying "Here, Lieutenant, you will need these glasses. I won't." I did not know then that he thought he would not need them because he planned to desert. As he was entrusted with our signal rockets, which he threw away, his desertion caused us a number of casualties the next day when our own artillery fire fell on us.

Finally the command came to advance again, and the line moved forward by rushing a few paces and falling prone. A few yards to my right a group of men were struck either by an exploding shell or a machine-gun volley; I saw three of them fall, twist and turn, and then lie motionless in grotesque positions. In several rushes my platoon reached the patch of woods referred to above, but only half the line was covered by it, the other half extending into the open. The units to our right appeared to have broken the German line as they suddenly moved forward rapidly and plunged into the woods on the crest of the hill; enemy fire slackened on our front. As we entered the little patch of woods we found we could advance standing up because of the sheltered position and the diminishing German fire. As I was going forward on the edge of the woods, trying to keep my men in line, which was difficult because half of them were in the woods and half in the open, I saw an American soldier lying prone with his rifle thrust forward through a bush as if he were about to fire. I hailed him, saying, "What outfit do you belong to, partner?" Receiving no reply and noticing he was not firing, I knelt by him and saw that he was dead; he had a gaping hole in his temple. We found another dead American nearby whom one of my men recognized as a private from Company K; both men probably had been killed only a minute or two before. I do not know how they happened to get in front of us, unless the battalion's line had become ragged and some units or groups were far in advance of others.

Companies K and M plunged into the woods after the fleeing Germans, capturing large numbers of prisoners and a battery of artillery. Company I on the right was having plenty of trouble, for it had taken a German trench and found itself in the peculiar position of being attacked from both the front and rear of the trench, and the men had to fire from both sides, which they did, beating off the enemy attack. Company L tried to maintain its line and advance into the woods in order, and it was well we did, because our company was well under control and this turned out to be the means of saving a victory from being turned into a disastrous defeat. If our company had rushed into the woods as did Companies K and M, helterskelter after the retreating Germans, who were falling back rapidly and in good order, there would have been no organized resistance to meet the German counterattack that soon came. The support battalion was too far behind to assist us. Events showed that Company L saved the day and that my platoon occupied the key position in the second phase of the first day's fighting.

As mentioned, the battalion front became ragged, and Company K on our right moved ahead and disappeared into the big woods beyond us. Bullets were still flying, but shellfire had decreased, probably because the Germans were retreating and the artillery did not have the range. I led my platoon, still in skirmish line, cautiously into the big woods from which the Germans had just retreated, and we came on a dead German lying on the ground, shot through the head by Lieutenant Kinkel of K Company, who in turn had been shot in the head by the German but not killed; as we came up the lieutenant was being led off by two of his men. But as we advanced into the woods, which became thicker with underbrush, everything seemed in confusion so far as Company K was concerned. Groups of men were wandering about the woods as if lost, and I learned later that others, without order or command, were pursuing the Germans through the woods. The company's officers had let things get out of control. Company M had so many casualties that it was scattered and disorganized, yet not as badly as Company K. Company I was under control but had all it could handle on the right near Ormont Woods.

Underbrush was so thick I had to form the platoon in single file in order to keep the men together, and not knowing what was before me and having lost touch with the rest of the company I halted the platoon and sent a runner to find Lieutenant Grassey. While waiting I sent out scouts ahead. The runner soon returned, having located the rest of the company, with the exception of the first platoon, halted a short distance on our left. He brought a message from Grassey for me to remain where

90

I was until I received further orders. There was a road a short distance ahead from which we could get a view of the valley on our left toward the Germans, and I led my platoon onto the road to wait for orders. Bullets were whistling dangerously about, so I had the men lie prone in the road. While waiting we heard a rifle shot a few yards away; I investigated and found that a man from Company K had shot himself in the arm so he would be sent to the rear.

We had been in this position about ten minutes when Lieutenant Grassey rushed up the road from the direction of the German retreat. He was excited and wanted to know where Lieutenant Derrickson was with his platoon; he said he was scouting ahead in the woods and was fired on from a German machine-gun nest, and a man accompanying him was shot through the arm. Grassey sent several men in search of Derrickson, with orders for him to move forward at once and attack the machine gun. The messengers hardly had disappeared in the woods when Grassey turned to me and said, "Lawrence, I can't wait for Derrickson. I wanted your platoon in reserve but you will have to clear out that machine-gun nest. Start at once. Here, take Stone. He will guide you to it."

Sergeant Meier told me later that when he heard Grassey give the command his, Meier's, teeth chattered so that his helmet beat a tattoo on his head. After Grassey gave the command he disappeared in search of Derrickson.

I called my three sergeants together and explained my plan. Meier was to take two squads and work around to the right and attract attention with grenade and rifle fire, while Mattson was to do the same with two squads on the left. I was to take the remaining two squads with Janz and rush the nest from the front. I took inventory of our ammunition and was disturbed to learn that we had no rifle or hand grenades; if the guns of a machine-gun nest have a good field of fire, which they usually have, it is difficult to take one without great loss of life unless rifle and hand grenades are used. A rifle grenade, fired from a cup fastened on the muzzle of an ordinary rifle, has a range of 210 yards, and the trajectory is in the shape of a semicircle and it will drop into the nest. Two or three well-placed grenades usually will do a great deal of good. Two men then spoke up and said they had seen some grenades along the road behind us and could get them and be back in two or three minutes, and I sent them off, and shortly afterward another man said he had seen some grenades. That sounded like too many rifle grenades along the road, for I had not seen any, and it occurred to me that the boys were trying to avoid the fight ahead. I did not let the third man go. The first two did not appear again until the fight was over; they were "lost" in the woods; I did not attempt to punish them because they did better next time and turned out to be good soldiers.[6]

The foregoing events occurred in less time than it takes to tell about them. It was hardly five minutes from the time Grassey gave me orders to make the attack until my platoon was moving forward. Without grenades I decided to make the attack with rifle and bayonet, and told the guide, Stone, to lead on. Then I received the astonishing reply that he did not know where any machine-gun nest was and that all he knew was that he had encountered Grassey running through the woods. I said, "Lead us to where you think Grassey had been." He said he did not know, but agreed that he could guess as to the general direction from which Grassey had come. "Lead on," I said. "Let's go."

We struck off at a brisk pace, down the narrow, crooked road, through the thick woods. Stone and I were in the lead, about twenty-five yards in advance, with the platoon following in column of twos. We had not gone far when bullets began to whine, and all at once American soldiers appeared, running through the woods, which were full of Germans. I passed two men standing behind trees and firing ahead, and one shouted, "Don't go down there, Lieutenant, the Boches are coming." Some of the men were running headlong, others would run a few paces and turn and fire in the direction from which they were retreating. This proved to be the remnant of Company K's line that had been broken by a counterattack and was being driven back in disorder. I could not see the pursuers because of the thick woods, but quickly realized that I had more than a machine-gun nest to deal with.

I decided to move on a little farther, hoping to ascertain the strength of the enemy, and had no idea he was so close at hand. As Stone and I turned a bend in the road we were startled to see a large body of Germans in the road ahead. I must have had only one or two glances at them but saw a lot in that short time: there was a group of men, presumably officers, studying what appeared to be a map in the hands of one of them. Several soldiers were standing around, leaning on rifles, and thirty or forty more men were in column on the road. Our sudden appearance electrified them into activity.

Stone saw them first, made one exclamation— "Boches!"—and gave me a shove that caused me to trip and fall in the bushes on the side of the road. He fled precipitously, and we did not find him for three weeks, when he was arrested and later convicted for desertion in the face of the enemy and sentenced to five years in

Leavenworth. My fall probably saved my life, however, as the rifle fire that followed passed over me. I had a glance at a German kneeling and aiming in my direction. I jumped to my feet, somewhat concealed by the bushes, fired two shots from my pistol at the Germans, and turned and ran with speed through the woods toward my men. The bullets whistled, but none struck me. I ran into the road after it had made a bend out of sight of the Germans, and saw my men standing in the road startled at Stone's rapid retreat to the rear and the rifle fire ahead. When they saw me burst out of the woods at a high rate of speed they did not wait for a command and turned as one man and beat a hasty but orderly retreat up the road. I overtook them a few yards in advance of the pursuing Germans, where a narrow-gauge railroad crossed our path, and managed to halt them and form a line with the men lying prone behind the railroad, which afforded a small measure of protection. Several were wounded by our pursuers before they could fall behind the railroad. One man was shot through both legs and fell on the side of the railroad toward the enemy, and lay there conscious, with the fire of both sides passing a few inches over his body. He pleaded for us to pull him in, but we could not reach the four feet to him without exposing ourselves to certain death.

Fifteen or twenty men from the scattered Company K joined us as we rushed for the railroad track, and we found fifteen or twenty more men behind the track when we got there, welcome reinforcements, for we did not get behind the track a second too soon, because the Germans were right on us. The instant the men were in position they fired a volley with deadly effect into the onrushing Germans, who were fifteen yards away. Although we could not see them well for the thick underbrush, I knew we were doing execution. Horrible screams of pain rent the air from the German side. Their piercing, bloodcurdling cries startled me; I feared we had fired on some of our men intermingled with the Germans and they were screaming to us to hold up. Again I thought we had killed some women, for we had heard wild stories about the Germans having women soldiers in their ranks. Neither assumption was correct, as we learned a little later; the screams came from dying German machine gunners of the 102d Saxon Regiment.

At the first opportunity I hurried two messengers back for reinforcements and ammunition. As I lay prone behind the railroad observing my line as far as I could, the men hotly exchanging deadly fire with the enemy in the woods fifteen or twenty yards away, I noticed a few interesting sidelights that later appeared to be amusing. A man named Gilbert, a few yards from me, had a rifle grenade that he clumsily was trying to fire. I do not know where he got it; there was not one in the platoon when we started down the road after the supposed machine-gun nest; finally he got it into the cup on the muzzle of his rifle and to my horror and before I could stop him he fired it straight up; I drew up in a knot waiting for it to fall on us, and it fell a few yards behind us with a loud crash, fortunately without damage. I noticed that the man next to me was cocking his rifle and pulling the trigger vigorously, but the rifle was not firing—it was not loaded. I stretched my leg around and gave him a kick, which seemed to bring him to his senses. I noticed that the two Heiser brothers, not over eighteen and twenty years old, were operating a Chauchat automatic rifle vigorously and apparently with deadly effect; one was firing the gun, while the other fed the ammunition.[7] It did not take them long to exhaust their ammunition at the rate they were firing, and when the last round was gone they tossed their gun aside, jerked out their .45 automatic pistols, and carried on with them. On the end of the line to the left of me I saw a big Company K sergeant, who I later learned was named Lavender, moving back and forth on his hands and knees keeping order on that end of the line.

Realizing that our ammunition was running low, and with no supply in sight, I decided to rush the Germans with the bayonet and passed the word down the line to watch for the signal. I caught Sergeant Lavender's eye, gave the signal, and we leaped forward. Only Lavender, about ten other men, and I leaped forward. We plunged into the woods for a few yards but had to beat a hasty retreat. Corporal Ernest Becker was badly wounded in this rush. I got far enough to see that the German advance position had been forced back and their line was thirty or fifty yards from us.

As we rushed forward I became separated from the other men and found myself alone. About ten yards ahead a bearded German officer stepped from behind a tree. I jumped behind another tree and covered him with my pistol. He stood out boldly, speaking to me in German, and thinking he wanted to surrender I stepped from behind my tree and motioned for him to come to me. He shook his head angrily and motioned me to him. We fired at each other about the same time. He did not hit me, and I do not know whether I hit him.[8]

As we fell back to our line I saw reinforcements coming down the road led by Fred Sexton, who had about thirty men from Company M. I ran to greet him and pointed out the position I wanted him to take. With the reinforcements and after Sexton was in position we must have had about 120 men, allowing for killed and wounded. I realized we could not hold the line with ammunition exhausted, and again it seemed there was nothing to do but rush the enemy. While I was making plans with Sergeant Lavender a soldier shouted, "Look, Lieutenant, look!" and pointed off to our left rear. Across a valley on a hill beyond, about half to three-quarters of a mile, we saw German infantry advancing toward us in line over a long front. They were advancing by short, irregular rushes—with care, thereby making a poor target.

★ VIII ★
A NEW LINE

Lawrence's men were a pickup group, but he had about 120, a considerable force. When he saw the German reinforcements advancing from afar he decided to take on his present opponents close at hand, while they were manageable. He and his men surged from behind the railroad track and into the woods and chased the Germans downhill and into a field. He then had to establish a new line, ideally behind a natural barrier that would protect his men in the woods. Here was a test of ingenuity, and he seized the ideal place a short distance up the hill. The decision was cool-headed, one of those acts by a small unit commander that with countless similar acts elsewhere brought victory to the American side in the Meuse-Argonne.

T he situation was serious, for I did not know where the rest of the battalion was. I had parts of three of the four companies with me. I did not know whether Company I had been broken up, as Company K had, and Derrickson, who had the first platoon of Company L, was supposed to support me and had not come up. None of the officers of the batallion except Sexton and I were on hand. Our part of the battle had gotten bigger and bigger. All the Germans attacking on our front must have been up by this time, and we had gotten reinforcements.

I passed the word down the line, gave the signal, and we went over again, with the same experience—all the men did not get up. Lavender and I rushed back and with strong language and other persuasion got the men up and in line, and we rushed forward in fairly good formation through the woods. Lavender with his rifle at "carry," bayonet fixed, of course, leaped ahead of the line and rushed alone twenty or thirty yards ahead. He was an inspiration to the men. I rushed forward and overtook him, and he and I reached the German line together.

For a while my observations were quite limited; I saw only what was immediately before me in the thick woods. My men and the Germans mingled in the thick underbrush, man to man. The struggle was brief, for the Germans began to fall back, disappearing in the woods, our men in pursuit. Lavender and I were the first to reach the Germans, and we picked out two riflemen that were side by side. Lavender lunged with his bayonet at the one on the left, who jumped aside and fled into the woods.[1] The other one hesitated for a split second, then turned to follow his comrade, and I fired at him with my pistol, the bullet striking just above the ear and tearing off the top half of his head; he crumpled to the ground, a gruesome sight—I saw him in the spot where he fell, four days later. The Germans fled down the hill, through the woods, and into an open field at the foot of the hill. Here our line halted, the men knelt, coolly took aim, and fired round after round at the fleeing Germans. The execution was heavy; thirty or forty were shot down, most of them killed. As I look back on the scene it is horrible, but then, while the heat of battle was upon us, it was thrilling. The Germans that were struck would leap into the air and fall to the ground writhing and twisting. Some would crawl a few yards and lie still. We did not kill them all, and most of them reached their trench and disappeared.[2]

I promptly began organizing my line. We withdrew a short distance up the hill, through the thick woods to a path that ran parallel to the line we faced. The path afforded the only opening in the underbrush and was bordered on the side toward the Germans by a rise of about a foot, affording somewhat of a makeshift breastwork. The field of fire was poor, as just in front of us the underbrush was so thick we could see only a few feet, but the ground in front of us was so heavily wooded and broken with deep ravines that the enemy could not approach us without great difficulty and without making enough noise to warn us. It was a position that could only be held with a concentration of men on the alert, as the ear and not the eye had to be depended upon. The line crossed the road that ran into the German lines and on which Stone and I had stumbled into the German advance. On the left the line ran down the hill to the edge of the woods, then turned almost at a right angle to the rear, where it stopped. There was a wide gap between our left and the right of the nearest unit, which I later learned was Derrickson's platoon.

Before I had completed my line the commander of Company I, Lieutenant McMahon, Sergeant Sweeten of M Company, and Grassey rushed up excited. Sweeten was waving his postol in the air, shouting, "Don't get excited, don't get excited!" Grassey, McMahon, and I conferred and decided that while the line we had taken had a poor field of fire it was the best we could do under the circumstances. It remained the most advanced position of the 113th Infantry for eight days, in spite of vigorous counterattacks, continuous and murderous

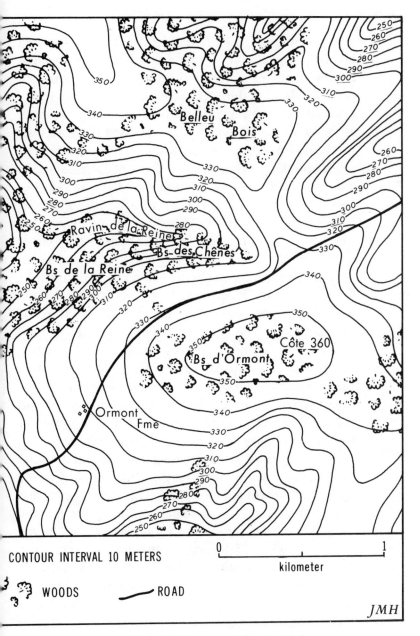

CONTOUR INTERVAL 10 METERS

0   1

kilometer

WOODS   ROAD

JMH

Contours of Bois de la Reine and Bois des Chênes

artillery fire, and daily raids by airplanes. Grassey and McMahon decided to leave me in command of this part of the line, now manned by about six depleted platoons—mine (third, Company L), all that was left of Company K, and several incomplete squads of Company M. None of the Company K officers was on hand; two had been wounded, one lost his mind temporarily from fright and fled to the rear, and the captain remained in a dugout, winning for himself the nickname of "Dugout Pete." The lieutenant, Young, who fled to the rear, mistook me for a German in his ravings and nearly shot me before I could convince him otherwise. All of Company M's officers had been killed or wounded except Fred Sexton, and he was killed the next night.[3]

It was now pitch dark, and I worked for several hours consolidating the line and trying to keep the men awake. The gap on our left worried me, and I decided to send four men as far into it as they could go and maintain touch with the main line. I selected the four and told them to create two outposts, two men in each, but the men balked, pleading with me not to send them into that dark gap where the German line was supposed to be close. To make matters worse, shells began to fall. I insisted they must go, and feeling that I should not send men where I would not go myself I told them I would go and help them get located; this heartened them, and I led off and they reluctantly followed. We groped around in the darkness until we found shell holes for the men to crawl in. I felt sorry for these men; the German line was only a short distance, and they were in imminent danger of being detected by wandering patrols or an alert sentry; if the Germans had advanced, these men could not have escaped. The noise of their destruction, however, would have warned us. They told me next day that a patrol passed so close they could hear the Germans talking.

After ascertaining that the line was in shape, and warning the noncommissioned officers to keep the men awake, I decided to find our company headquarters and report to Lieutenant Grassey, and it was with much difficulty that I found Grassey's dugout in the darkness; we were in a thick woods with much underbrush and few paths. I picked my way cautiously in the general direction of the dugout. There was danger of encountering German patrols and being mistaken by wandering Americans for a German. I passed wounded men lying in the woods, and when they heard me stumbling through the bushes they cried out, "We are Americans. Water! Water! Water!" My canteen long since had been emptied, and I could do nothing for them. I found the dugout about a quarter of a mile from our line, and after spending about ten minutes in the dugout conversing with Grassey about our position I took one of the men stationed in the dugout to go with me and learn the way, and started back to the line. A short distance from the dugout I saw where a soldier had cached his overcoat, close to the path, and discovering that it fitted me, and not knowing if the owner was dead or alive, I took it. I needed one, not having one of my own. Reaching the line I sent the runner back to Grassey.[4]

Shortly after getting back I heard a commotion on the lower end of my line and found that our men had captured a German and were getting ready to kill him. He had been wounded, a bullet having passed through both cheeks, but he was standing erect. He was apprently about fifty years old and had a thick black beard. I drew my gun, rescued him from the men, and motioned for him to walk ahead of me, which he did with enthusiasm. I intended to take him to a dressing station and turn him over to the prisoners' detail, and had noticed that the dressing station was close to Grassey's dugout. Knowing the way, I made good time until I encountered an American patrol, which wanted to know what I was going to do with the prisoner. When I told them what I planned to do they remonstrated, and urged that I turn him over to them for proper disposal, which meant sudden death for the prisoner. He knew what the conversation was about and grasped me just above the hips from behind and held on with trembling hands. I refused to give up my prisoner and proceeded on my way. When we reached the dressing station I found it alive with activity, the surgeons doing what they could for suffering, wounded men. Those the doctors had finished with were either being brought out on stretchers to be carried to the ambulances waiting a mile away, or were being placed on the ground close by to be buried later. Arriving at the dugout entrance I called down that I had a wounded prisoner who needed attention, and one of the doctors replied, "Take him out and shoot him." Seeing that I could get no help I looked around and found an empty dugout and left him in it. Some Company L men were occupying a dugout close by, and I instructed them to keep an eye on the wounded prisoner. Next day when I reported to company headquarters I went to the dugout where I left my prisoner and found him still there, and sent a man in to bring him out. He looked as if he had suffered great pain during the night. Again I took him to the dressing station; they were not very busy so they agreed to fix him up. He gave me a grateful look when I left him. He was a little later sent to the rear with a detail of prisoners, and I was told he was in pretty good shape when he left.

Disposing of the prisoner I returned to the line through the dark, tangled, shell-torn woods, reeking with poison gas. The Germans now were shelling the woods with light artillery. I had the urge to dig a hole and crawl in it and stay, but picked my way back to the line and found things all right for the time being. I discovered what appeared to be a platform a few feet behind our line and decided to lie down and get a little rest. It was too dark to see any of the surroundings, and I soon fell asleep in spite of the desultory shell fire and the fact that some of the shells were exploding uncomfortably close. I awoke at dawn and sat up with a start when I discovered that I had been sleeping on the floor of what had been a house before it was destroyed by shellfire and was in full view of the German lines. I rolled off and took cover with the men, who were protected from sight by a thick screen of bushes. This was the morning of October 11, 1918.

The Germans had not yet found our line, although their patrols had been heard close by during the night; I had been compelled to instruct the men to hold their fire except in great emergency because our ammunition was nearly exhausted and I did not know when we would be supplied from the rear. It was well that we took that precaution, because our ammunition did not come up until late that night. I learned afterward that our battalion line was in the shape of a horseshoe and the Germans kept a barrage playing on the neck with such severity that no supply details could get through. Nor could details get back with the wounded.

Our supply company and company kitchens were stationed in a rather wide ravine a kilometer and a half behind us, and the barrage was between us and the ravine. These units were discovered in the ravine and shelled unmercifully with heavy artillery. Many men and horses were killed and wounded, and one kitchen and considerable other equipment and supplies destroyed. This added, to be sure, to our troubles up on the front line. The ravine thereafter was known as Death Valley.[5]

While the day of the eleventh was busy, no attacks were made by infantry on either side. Both sides seemed content to consolidate their lines and care for the wounded—except, however, the German artillery and airplanes, which did not seem to need rest and busied themselves blasting our position with light shells and machine-gun fire. About three o'clock that afternoon a plane flew over and sprayed our lines with machine-gun bullets, and thereafter the Germans knew where our lines were. I inspected that part of the line under my command from time to time and had my hands full even though no attack was made. The line, again, ran down a wooded hillside along a path, and the hill rose behind us to a height of about fifty feet. The most exposed part of our position was at the foot of the hill where my line stopped, for the battalion line there made a right-angle turn to the rear. During the night of the tenth, Company A had come up and taken position on our left, but it faced a direction at a right angle to the direction we faced, and our contact was not good; a gap remained for twenty-four hours.

Late in the afternoon Sergeant Meier of my platoon came to me on the upper end of the line and said excitedly, "Lieutenant, you will have to come down on the lower end of this line and take charge. There are Boches out in front of us. They have been firing at us all afternoon and I believe they are coming over and I don't know what to do." This was discomforting news, for we did not have enough ammunition to repel a determined attack. Meier and I worked our way cautiously down the line, crawling the last forty feet on hands and knees, and found the men on the point frightened but steady. They said the activity in no-man's-land had ceased shortly after Meier left. Here it was possible for the Germans to approach within a few yards without being seen; the point was a bad spot, and I did not blame the men for not wanting to stay there. I had to leave Meier, my most reliable sergeant, at this place all the time, and he had his hands full keeping his men in place, and the shortage of ammunition made matters worse.

I stayed on the point for about half an hour and then worked my way back toward my place on the center of the line, and on my way back a position occupied by two men attracted my attention. It was elevated, but protected by two large trees in front and large rocks on all sides; the position afforded an excellent view, over the tops of the nearby trees, of Belleu Bois where the Germans were in force. This was to our left and in the direction faced by Company A and the main part of Company L, our company. The men who occupied this post were North Carolinians and told me they had observed some activity on the edge of Belleu Bois across the valley. I had not been at the post but a few minutes when I saw a whole company of German infantry emerge from the woods and march parallel to the edge, out in the open; then they turned back into the woods. A machine gun mounted where we were could have done considerable execution, but we did not have a machine gun. Our ammunition was so low, and our position so isolated, that the Germans could pass by unmolested.

One of the North Carolinians told me that their post had been located by German snipers and they had to be very careful how they exposed themselves. While the German infantry company was marching by I was so absorbed in watching them that I unwittingly exposed myself; instantly a rifle barked and I felt a hot sting on my cheek as a sniper's bullet grazed it and struck a rock right by my head, throwing rock splinters in my face. I took cover immediately.

The next day, October 12, I did some sniping myself from this same spot. Late that afternoon I had stopped by to take a look into no-man's-land, and the two North Carolinians told me that a few minutes before they had detected a movement in the woods across no-man's-land where we had seen the Germans emerge from the woods the day before. I decided to stay there a while and watch, and borrowed the rifle of one of the men and waited. In a few minutes two Germans walked out in the open and looked over our way. One of the men and I each picked out a German, took careful aim, and fired almost simultaneously. Both Germans fell. The one I shot got up and I fired again, and he fell on his knees and disappeared. I do not know whether he was killed or crawled away.

Meanwhile the night of October 11-12 had proved exciting, as late in the night Meier came to me from his dangerous post, much disturbed, and said the Germans were moving up in force on our front that faced the tangled jungle of trees and underbrush and that he and his men could hear them placing machine guns in position and talking. Meier could speak German and said he heard a German say, "The Americans are not far away. We had better stop here."

We were not prepared to resist a strong attack with our scanty supply of ammunition and our single line of infantry, and I turned command of the line over to Lavender of Company K and picked my way through the darkness to Grassey's dugout some distance back and reported the situation. He immediately reported to battalion headquarters and asked for ammunition above all things, reinforcements, and artillery coverage. I returned to the line and took charge again, and in about an hour, much to our relief, a detail came up with an adequate supply of ammunition, which was quickly passed out. The corporal in charge brought word from Grassey that Company D was on the way, and I was particularly concerned about the gap between our left and Company A and also worried about our left where Meir was at the foot of the hill in an exposed position. We knew the Germans were very close to Meier's point, and I intended to have Company D take this part of the line and close the gap and relieve Meier and his men so they could strengthen the rest of my part of the line. Meier, incidentally, confessed to me that night, while I was with him for a few minutes, that he had not lived a model life and had been prone to get drunk quite often. He said he could now see the error of his ways and if God would let him live he would lead a model life and never taken another drink. God let him live, but Meier forgot his promise soon after we were relieved and he was out of danger.

After waiting for what seemed a lifetime for Company D to come up I sent a man back to look for them, as it would not be long until daybreak and we knew the Germans would attack as soon as it became light. My runner soon returned with information that Company D was in position about seventy-five yards directly behind us. I could not understand why they would take such a position without contacting the first line; they were not where they were needed. I hurried to their position, found the company commander who was a lieutenant, and explained the situation, and he was quite willing to move but said his company had been put there by Major Freeman, commander of the 1st Battalion, 113th Infantry, and Freeman would have to give permission for the company to move. He asked me to get back to the major's dugout with him and explain the situation. We found the major in a deep dugout comfortably stretched out on a bunk. There were three or four other officers in the dugout with him. The lieutenant told the major that I said his company was in the wrong position.

The major became furious and bellowed, "Lieutenant, what do you mean by leaving your command? Get out of here and get back there immediately."

"Major," I said, "let me explain to you the condition of the front line."

He glowered at me and said, "I don't know who you are and don't give a damn. Both of you get out of here."

Major Freeman was of that breed that tries to cover up shortcomings with loud talk; he was afraid to inspect his lines. When we left the dugout one of the officers who was with Freeman told him, as I learned later, that he "should have listened to that lieutenant because he has been in command of that part of the line ever since it was established and knows what he is talking about." The major discovered his mistake the next day while the battle was raging and had the company moved under fire. This act of his was responsible for the death of a number of good men, including the lieutenant who accompanied me to the dugout.

★ IX ★
HOLDING OUT

Unnerving artillery fire—shrieking, thudding shells, eardrum-splitting explosions, shrapnel and dirt everywhere—preceded the German attack. Fire also came from "shorts," friendly guns; Lawrence found his line shelled from front and rear. With difficulty the Americans then beat off the attackers. Afterward they settled down to what proved to be six more days of holding out on the advance line, huddled in mud and rain, seldom with hot food, often with no food at all.

Just before daybreak of October 12, 1918, pandemonium broke loose when the Germans started a severe barrage of artillery fire, sweeping our line from end to end. They had the range. Our artillery replied but did not have the range; we were farther advanced than they thought and their fire fell short and did as much damage to our line as did the German fire, and perhaps more. We were caught in both barrages, and it was terrible—shells coming from front and rear at the same time, striking the same line, the American barrage heavier than that of the Germans because our artillery was using larger guns. I was on the front line with the men, lying

111

prone behind a mound of earth about a foot high that bordered the path along which our line ran, and our men were in line about three feet apart, on my right Corporal Stuart of Company K and on my left two privates, also of Company K. There were no Company K officers anywhere, and most of the remnants of the company were with my command. One of the privates on my left was a boy of about eighteen, badly frightened, a pitiful sight, drawn up in a knot, trembling like a leaf, whimpering. His behavior got on Corporal Stuart's nerves, and he sat up on the mound of earth that was our breastworks, with his back toward the Germans, and upbraided the boy profanely. I expected to see Stuart shot to pieces any second, but he was not touched.[1]

The Germans now opened up with machine-gun and rifle fire and our men replied vigorously with rifles and Chauchats.

The shelling, which continued, was terrible, particularly from the American guns. I heard a big shell coming from our side that I knew was going to hit close to where I was; its screech became louder and louder and then ended in a deafening roar as it struck a large tree under which we were lying. It struck about ten feet up, cutting the tree in two, and the upper part fell straight down, striking the man on my left (not the boy) as he lay prone, on one leg above the knee, practically cutting his leg from his body. Another American shell exploded close by, showering us with dirt and rocks. Then two German shells hit the mound in front of us and showered us with debris from that side. One hit within two or three feet of my head, but I was protected by the mound. As soon as we recovered from the shock, Stuart and I put a tourniquet on the stump of the wounded man's leg. He was conscious and asked if the doctor was coming, and I told him, "Yes, he will be here in a few minutes." But I saw that a doctor could do him no good, and he died in a few minutes. There were, of course, no doctors around at such a time.

We beat off the Germans. I do not know how long it took. They finally withdrew and the shelling subsided. Our casualties were many. I do not know how many men were killed and wounded because most of those under my command in this fight were from other companies and I never learned the details of the casualties. No one in my platoon was killed in the fight, but several were wounded and a number were shell-shocked. Meier escaped whole but was showered with debris knocked up by exploding shells. When our artillery began to fall short we should have sent up signal rockets immediately, but we could not do that because our deserter, First Sergeant Murphy, had thrown them all away when he fled from the battle.

Although we repulsed the German attack, the enemy withdrew only forty yards from our line and took up a strong position. We faced the Boches in this position for six days, and it was an extremely difficult position to hold and the strain on the men was terrific. Casualties were many, for we were lying prone or crouched in shell holes, and anyone who exposed himself in the daytime was sure to draw fire. The Germans were similarly situated, and we fired at their slightest movement. No one from either side dared venture into the narrow no-man's-land, day or night.

Late in the afternoon a sudden burst of machine-gun fire came from our right, and a man close by me groaned and grasped his right arm with his left hand, for he had been struck in the shoulder. A sergeant reported that several other men had been hit, farther to the right. I got up to investigate and the bullets whistled by. We were puzzled for a while as to their origin, but soon learned that our line was being enfiladed by machine guns mounted on a hill to our right. For a space of about fifty yards this fire swept right down our line. For this part of the line we had to execute a dangerous adjustment and move back a few yards and dig in quickly, all done while the men were lying prone so as not to expose themselves to the fire in front.

Late in the afternoon I went back to company headquarters to report to Grassey, a dangerous trip to and from the line, a trip I did not make more often than I had to. While the woods screened me from sight on the ground, the danger from artillery fire and gas was great, as the Germans shelled this area continuously. I thought that each trip I made from the front line would be the last, and on this particular trip I had to flatten out on the ground three or four times as the German 77s screamed at me and with a loud "swish" struck the ground with a deafening roar. Grassey told me after I reached the dugout that he wanted me to bring my platoon in after dark and join the rest of Company L on that part of the line assigned it, and said that Company K should take full responsibility for the part of the line my platoon had assisted in taking and defending.

A feud had sprung up between Grassey and Captain Staley of Company K. They occupied neighboring dugouts, and while Grassey's was close to his command, Staley's was far from his. He did not visit his line. I was the only officer to whom his men could look for instructions. As stated before, the position of our 3d Battalion was in the shape of a horseshoe: the left side was held by Company L (our company) and a support company, Company A; the toe was held by remnants of Companies K and M and by my platoon of Company L; the right side by Company I. Only one ration detail had gotten through the German barrage since we had gone

114

over the top on October 10, and we had been practically three days without food and scarcely no water and very little sleep—and as I learned later, this was just the beginning. Company L got no food from this first detail, and Grassey said Captain Staley had taken our share. I was with Company K, however, when its rations, and probably L's share, were passed out, and I at least had one meal, though of questionable quality, after the morning of October 10.

While I was at his dugout Grassey told me I had been recommended for a Distinguished Service Cross.

Captain Staley was not pleased when I informed him I had orders to withdraw from his part of the line, and said he had no officers and needed me. He told me to tell Grassey that he, Staley, outranked him and I was to stay on the line. He said, incidentally, that I had been recommended for the Croix de Guerre.

Grassey raved at length when I delivered Staley's message, and ordered me to withdraw my platoon as soon as it was dark enough and to station the men in the partly destroyed dugouts in the vicinity of his headquarters. I was to report back to his dugout and get some rest. I had not slept but three or four hours in the last four days, though there probably were times when I dozed for a few minutes during the comparative lulls in the almost continuous heavy firing.

Captain Staley's confinement to his dugout, a German-built, concrete dugout, became known throughout the battalion, and he took the unusual precaution of having two sentries at the entrance at all times; he probably thought a German patrol might slip through the lines and raid his dugout. Someone, I suspect it was Grassey, persuaded Lieutenant Bradbury, commanding the one-pound cannon platoon of our regiment, to mount a gun on the concrete roof of Stone's dugout. A one-pound

115

cannon is a vicious little weapon and very effective in breaking up machine-gun nests, but they are hated by the infantry for they were so effective that the enemy artillery gave them special attention. The crews operating these guns would take up a position, fire as many rounds as they could before the enemy got the range, and then scamper for cover, leaving the infantry to catch the artillery fire. Whenever they came around our part of the line we would chase them away. And so when Bradbury's gun opened up, Staley was but a split second coming to the surface. He swished out of the dugout and all but assaulted the gun crew. He drove them away in short order. He had hardly regained the safety of his dugout when the German artillery began "feeling" for Bradbury and his gun. Grassey enjoyed the episode immensely.[2]

I spent the night of October 12 in Grassey's dugout and got some much-needed sleep. The Germans had occupied the dugout a few days before, and four or five rifles and bayonets were found in it when Grassey took possession. It was occupied by Grassey, Al Roland the acting first sergeant, Bill Batt the supply sergeant, Casey the company clerk, and Red Morgan who was a desperado and whom Grassey preferred to have where he could see him and who acted as runner or messenger; there also was another runner. I learned from the men in the dugout that the 26th (Yankee) Division had moved up behind us and was camped where we had been when we "went over the top." We were all praying that this division would relieve us, for many of our men were showing signs of cracking under the strain. We had been under continuous shellfire, rifle and machine-gun fire, gassing, attacks by planes, no food, and only what muddy rainwater we could get from holes in the ground. It was drizzling rain and cold, the men were wet to the skin, cold, hungry, thirsty, some of them frightened, many sick from the gas, all in dread of the never-ceasing, screaming, crashing shells. The strain was terrible.

Early the next morning, October 13, Lieutenant Derrickson suddenly appeared at the dugout door, stood there for a moment as if dazed, and blurted out: "Grassey, what are you going to do about it? Something has got to be done."

"What's the matter with you?" said Grassey. "Are you crazy?"

"The men are all crazy and I am going crazy," replied Derrickson. "The Minenwerfers are blowing us to pieces."[3]

"I will send Lawrence down to relieve you if you can't stand it," said Grassey.

That did not sound so good to me.

Derrickson then said, with much dignity, "I will never desert my men."

"All right," said Grassey. "Go on back."

Derrickson turned and left the dugout and picked his way back to his battered line.

But my stay in the dugout did not last long, for the 114th Infantry was making an attack on Ormont Woods where the Germans were strongly entrenched on our right and enfilading our line. Company A of our regiment was withdrawn from its position in our line between Company L and Company K and detailed to take part in the attack on Ormont Woods. Grassey was informed of this move and ordered to stretch Company L to the right and fill the gap vacated by Company A, and I was thereupon given the remnants of my platoon and one squad from Company K and ordered to fill the gap at once. Company A moved out so fast it was gone before I could find its position. Stumbling around in the shell-torn jungle through which our lines ran was not safe, for the terrain was under continuous German fire and there was danger of getting in front of our own men. I halted my pieced-up platoon a comparatively safe distance back and took a young corporal, H. M. Rennard, and scouted ahead to look for the position. It was getting dark, and the Germans might locate the gap; it had to be found and contacts made on each end quickly.

Rennard was a fine-looking young fellow, eighteen years old, straight and tall, who had falsified his age when he joined the army because he then was under the legal age. It seemed a shame for boys like him to be in this holocaust; he should have been in some college preparing himself for a useful career. There were too many boys in this war on all sides.

One would not have expected Rennard to have had murderous inclinations, and yet he did have. A detachment of about six German prisoners halted near Grassey's dugout on their way to the rear, after we had driven the Germans from the woods on October 10. Their guard was holding them there to join other detachments to form a larger detail. One German had a slight but apparently painful scalp wound and seemed to be groaning unduly, and it annoyed Rennard, who was standing close by. Rennard ordered the German to quiet down, and when he failed to do so Rennard drew his pistol. Grassey, noting the incident, commanded Rennard to put up his gun and keep away from the prisoners. As Grassey turned his back to walk away, a loud report rang out; when he turned he saw the German stretched out on the ground dead and Rennard walking off nonchalantly returning his pistol to the holster.

This was the man I selected to scout ahead with me. He and I picked our way hurriedly through the thick underbrush, realizing we were in serious danger of being shot by both the Germans and our own men. We reached the edge of the woods toward the German line, and a bullet whistled uncomfortably close to our heads. We paused, and suddenly Rennard raised his arm and pointed ahead. "I see him, Lieutenant," he said. I peered over his shoulder. Suddenly there was a loud report, a light thud, and Rennard sank to the ground. I dropped instantly and flattened out, then looked to Rennard. The bullet had entered between his eyes and come out through the back of his head; I could do nothing for him. The German sniper had the range and I was armed with only a pistol, and I did not tarry long. Rennard had a number of boyhood friends in the platoon, and they were disheartened and depressed by his death.

When I returned to the platoon I deployed it where it was and after some difficulty made contact on the left with Derrickson's platoon and the right with Company K. We closed the gap, but with a very thin line. I threatened to place the corporal in charge of the Company K squad under arrest for his repeated attempts to desert his position for a safer one farther to the rear; I had to keep close watch all through the night to hold him and his squad in position.

All through that night of October 13, and the next day, October 14, the Germans shelled our lines. We had dug in as deeply as we could, into the hard, rocky soil, but most of the men crouched in shell holes if they were not too far off the line, concealing themselves by covering the holes with brush. The Germans were not far off. We could not see them because they too were concealed in holes, but at the least sound from us they made themselves known. A man's equipment striking a

119

rock as he turned in his hole, or too much noise in digging deeper holes, would start the methodical put-put-put of the German machine guns, which sounded terribly loud and frightfully close. A gun fired at one, of course, sounds close even though it may be some distance. We would reply with Chauchats and rifles. Then it would all stop at once, only to be renewed farther down the line; a slight sound or a slight move would set off the firing. The artillery never seemed to tire, and the screaming, screeching shells would tear at our ragged line, snapping nerves, taking out a man here and there; sometimes one of two men occupying a shell hole would be mangled while his partner would not be scratched. The smell coming from an exploding shell is terrible, not a bad odor particularly but acrid, ominous, and frightfully suggestive. A shrill screech, a deafening explosion, flying dirt, shell fragments—the acrid smell; it missed us that time, but there is another one behind it, another, and another, and so on, for hours; then a pause for an hour or so, or less, then another barrage, and so on ad infinitum.

The men couldn't stand much more of this. We had had it for four days and were hungry, hollow-eyed, exhausted. Some of them were losing their minds. Monahan, one of our best sergeants, had broken, his nervous system shattered, and was up in Grassey's dugout whimpering like a baby; he was a fine young fellow and a brave soldier, but there was a limit to human endurance.

Two boys, Sullivan and Pulveritis, were my runners. Sullivan, a nineteen-year-old Irish boy, was blown twenty feet from the floor of a barn, up into the rafters, when a shell struck the barn in which he was sleeping when the division was in Alsace; he landed in the hay, and his only injury was a black eye. Pulveritis was a likeable little

German-born kid, not over nineteen. I thought Grassey should know that our line was dangerously thin and that the Germans before us were very active, and sent word back by Sullivan and Pulveritis and instructed them to return immediately, for I was expecting an attack and needed them on hand to warn headquarters; I sent them together because I wanted them to learn the way. An hour passed and they did not come back, and I became anxious, for I had to establish contact. The only other man available was the platoon sergeant, Dunne, and he did not know the way, so I left him in charge and went myself. Grassey hadn't seen Sullivan or Pulveritis. A search among the half-destroyed dugouts in the vicinity produced a result, for they were found sleeping in one of them. Grassey drew his gun and threatened to shoot both of them. They protested hysterically that they were not yellow—they were worn out, dead tired. He sent them sobbing back to the hell from which they had sought to steal a little relief. Pulveritis had hardly gotten back to his foxhole when a shell exploded almost in his face, ripped his steel helmet open, and tore off part of his scalp and face. He lived.

The platoon sergeant, Dunne, was a brave, nice-looking young fellow, an Italian whose real name was Dundero. During a lull in the shelling that night I took him back to headquarters for him to learn the way. We proceeded cautiously, our bodies bent low, up a narrow path through the shell-torn, dark woods. We came to a dead man lying across the path and I said to Dunne, "When you come to this dead man, you turn sharp to the right." Incidentally he was the man I had shot four days before. Dunne told me later that the incident so unnerved him that it took him several days to get over it.

In the afternoon of October 15, Grassey called me back to the dugout and turned over the part of the line I had established to Derrickson.

I was glad to get back to the dugout, where I could get some sleep, but had hardly stretched out on a filthy German bunk when word came that Lieutenant Mims and Sergeant Anderson, who occupied the same shell hole on the line, had both been hit by a shell and badly wounded; Anderson had a leg cut off, and a piece of shell had entered Mims' stomach and passed through his body. I was off again, ordered to take command of Mims's platoon. It was dark and raining, but I found the location without much difficulty and crawled in a shallow hole with the platoon sergeant, Ruddy, and stretched out with him in the mud and water in the bottom of the hole which was about twelve inches deep, five feet long, and three feet wide, a very uncomfortable place in the rain and cold.[4]

On October 17, Grassey sent word that Derrickson had been wounded and directed me to leave Ruddy in command and take over Derrickson's men, the first platoon and the remnant of my platoon. With Derrickson incapacitated I was the only Company L officer left on the line, and had "trench foot" so bad that I could hardly walk.[5] I hobbled up to the dugout and found that Derrickson was not seriously wounded but was suffering from exhaustion and shock. Leaning heavily on Red Morgan, the red headed ex-Sing-Sing inmate, I hobbled down to the shell hole Derrickson had occupied. One of Derrickson's runners was Leo Bednarkiewicz, better known as Bozo, and he and I occupied the same foxhole. He was in a bad way, for the long strain had about broken him; he was shell-shocked and half starved. I had hardly joined him in the hole when he began pleading for me to let him go back to the dugout for just five minutes; he said five minutes' relief from that hell of Minenwerfer shells, machine-gun fire, and gas would be like going to heaven. I felt like saying to Bozo, "Let's both go back," and finally let him go back for thirty minutes, which turned out to be two hours, and I had to crawl back to the dugout and get him out.

After dark I inspected the line and found that the men were holding on determinedly but were in bad shape—hungry, wet, caked from head to foot with mud and filth, suffering from dysentery caused by the gas (the woods reeked with gas, and many of the men were careless about using their masks and consequently were affected before they realized it). When night came I heard someone slipping through the bushes, quickly investigated, and found one of my men attempting to slip to the rear; the poor fellow was like Bozo, wanting a few minutes of relief from the hell on the line. This kept up all night, making it necessary for me to patrol the line, at considerable risk; I would drive one man back to his position and another would try to slip by.

October 18, the ninth day of continuous action, again saw little food, save some cold, foul-smelling hash one day, some canned tomatoes another, and French black bread and molasses another—the bread was full of holes, and we poured the molasses on the bread and it trickled through the holes and spread out in our whiskers and mingled there with the mud and other accumulations.

Early that morning the Germans shelled our lines heavily. They had the range better and made more hits, and were coming closer than usual. Bozo and I flattened out in our hole, gritted our teeth, clenched our hands, and drew our muscles rigid while shell after shell crashed close by. Corporal Froehner and another man occupied a hole next to ours, and we heard a big shell coming right toward us, screaming louder. I thought the end had come, and it exploded with a roar, shocking us with the impact. After a moment I realized I was not hit. I spoke to Bozo—he was all right. Over in the next hole Froehner's partner was missing. Froehner was lying on his back, his eyes as large as half dollars.

"Are you hurt, Froehner?" I asked.

He shook his head.

"Where is your partner?"

"He ran away," mumbled Froehner. "The shell," he explained, "knocked his foot off."

That sounded strange. How could he run away with one foot? I learned later that the shell took off all of his foot except the heel, enough for him to flee through the woods, where he was caught.

General Upton, our brigade commander, ordered our regiment to advance and attack the German position on this day, but rescinded the order when he learned the condition of the men. Captain Staley did us a good turn that day when he told the general he would not order his men, in their weakened condition, to make an assault on the German lines. This incident together with a few others cost Staley his commission, for he was forced by General Upton to resign.[6]

Then, during the morning, while the shelling was heavy, I heard the sweetest sound I ever listened to— an American battery of French 75-millimeter guns opened up just behind us. The ringing bark of those remarkable guns was music to our ears, and it meant that relief was near and the Germans would have something else to do besides shell us. Other American batteries opened, and the German fire slackened; the Americans had the range and were doing execution among the German gunners. We were tremendously encouraged. A little food at that moment would have done wonders, but we did not get it.[7]

Darkness came, and we settled down for another night of hell. About eight o'clock a large detail of men came down the hill from the rear, guided by Red Morgan and making entirely too much noise. Could this be the relief? Sure enough it was. Red reported that we were being relieved by the 102d Infantry, 26th Division—the Yankee Division, as it was called—from New England, and I was to report with my men to company headquarters.

★ X ★
RELIEF

*New Englanders of the 26th Division replaced the Blue
and Gray, the 29th, on the evening of October 18, and
no one was happier than Lawrence and his men. After
moving back, however, they were not out of danger,
which lessened only as they passed to the rear over a
period of several days.*

D ouse that light, buddy," one of my men said to one
of the relief who had just lighted a cigarette.

"What for?" asked the New Englander.

"You'll find out what for damn quick."

"You guys must think we ain't been on the front
before," the relief man said.

What with this cigarette-smoking and noise I knew
things would begin to happen very soon, so I got my
men out as quickly as possible. We were none too soon,
because the Germans opened up with all they had. We
learned later that the 102d Infantry was badly damaged
that night. They had to learn in their own way.

The 26th Division attacked the German lines next day
and were repulsed. They attacked a second time and
were driven back with heavy losses. They were ordered

to attack a third time, but the men had had enough for one day and refused. Next day they were reinforced by the 79th Division (Maryland and Pennsylvania) and attacked again, and this time drove the Germans back.[1]

When I got to headquarters Grassey and Derrickson were in the dugout explaining our position to the commanding officer of the company that relieved us, Captain Bell, who was young and capable looking.

We were soon on our way with our ragged remnants, feeling our way to the rear through the darkness and shellfire, a sorry-looking company as it hobbled out of the front line that night, less than half the strength that went in. We went out in single file, following our guide. My feet were paining me, and it was with difficulty that I kept up. As I recall we lost one man on the way out.

We were not being taken out of the battle, just retired from the front line to a reserve position in Death Valley about a mile and a half to the rear, the place where the supply company of our regiment was nearly annihilated. Here the other officers and I crowded into a dugout already full. I attempted to sleep on the floor in the aisle, as there were no bunks available, and every few minutes someone would step on me, so I had to give up the place. I found a spot where I could sit on a bench, but it was under dripping water from the roof; I took the spot and got some rest, in spite of the water. Next morning, October 19, we found we were stationed in the valley with a detachment of French heavy artillery that was shelling the Germans, and we amused ourselves by sitting behind the big guns and watching the shells leave the muzzles and disappear into the distance. The gunners amused themselves by giving commands in what they thought was English; they would give commands in that way and then look at us and laugh. It was comparatively safe to walk around in the valley, although it was shelled scatteringly at intervals. I noticed that many of the shells that fell in the valley were duds.

Late in the afternoon two men, hollow-eyed, covered with mud, ragged but indignant, came into the valley. They belonged to our company and had been overlooked when we withdrew. They were all that was left of their squad, and too well concealed for their own good. They served an extra day in the front line. "You guys are fine soldiers," a corporal said. "You were so well hidden your own sergeant thought you were captured. What have you been living on all these days, dead Germans?"

We spent the day leisurely in the valley, relieved to walk erect, even if we had to be alert and listen for shells coming our way. When we heard them coming we would dive into a dugout, if one was in reach; if not, into a shell hole. Drinking water was still scarce, but I used about a cupful from my canteen to shave and wash my face for the first time in over two weeks. That night we had more room in the dugout because some of the occupants moved out.

Next morning, October 20, I learned that regimental headquarters was in a neighboring valley, and several of us walked over to see if we could get the news and there found Blair, who was with headquarters. Much to my sorrow I learned that my best friend, Fred Sexton, was missing. After the other officers of Company M had been killed or wounded, Fred took command, and when inspecting his line one night he walked unwittingly into no-man's-land and was captured. We learned later from some prisoners that he was shot through the head with a pistol when he refused to give information. His body was found with one bullet hole through his head. Lenson Graves, my first buddy, had been killed, and now Fred Sexton. I learned from Blair of other casualties among my friends. Among those of our detail that left the training school together, Fred Sexton, "Uncle Bun" Bailey, and Running were killed, and Mims and John Wood were seriously wounded.[2]

Several of us climbed to the top of the hill and got in a trench that had been occupied a few days before, so as to observe the surrounding country. To the rear I saw three mounted men ride up to what appeared to be a headquarters dugout and enter. They left their horses tied at the dugout entrance, and while I stood looking at them and at nearby shellbursts a shell struck the horse in the middle, killing him but apparently not hurting the other two.[3]

Of all jobs that a soldier hates, that of policing— picking up trash—takes first place, and on October 21, while still in the valley, our pride was much hurt by being ordered to police the battlefield over which we had fought the first day of our heavy fighting. We were instructed to collect unexploded shells, bury dead men if any were found (they had been collected once), and also bury dead horses. If we saw a dead horse in the distance we carefully avoided him, for it was quite an undertaking to bury a horse in the hard, rocky soil, using only our hand shovels. This policing job was not only unpleasant and unmilitary but dangerous, for the area was still under shellfire; I had to dive into a shell hole a number of times. We finished the job the next day, October 22, without casualties; the only eventful incident was a row several of us had with a group of Frenchmen who returned to their dugout and found us helping ourselves from their keg of wine. We could not understand all they said, but there was no mistaking their gestures. One bearded Frenchman said disgustedly, "Americans, comrades, bah!" We did not like their attitude, and for a while it looked like there was going to be a bad fight. We cussed and glared at each other. Then they sauntered off one way and we sauntered off another.

Late in the afternoon of October 24 we received orders to fall in and marched over the hill toward the rear to the valley opening on the Meuse, called the Côte des Roches, the valley from which we had left on the morning of October 10 to go over the top. As we marched we passed the 114th Infantry coming up to make an attack that night. My heart went out to those boys; I knew where they were going, and what they were going into, and had a peculiar feeling of deep sympathy for them.

We spent all the next day, October 25, in the Côte des Roches, far enough back to camp in pup tents even though we were only a few yards behind several batteries of American artillery engaged in shelling the German lines with French 75s. It was here, this day, that we got a meal, quite an unusual experience, being served corned beef, bread, and coffee early in the morning. This was the first issue of food approaching a full meal in two weeks. Someone then announced that Mass was being held in an adjacent valley. When the announcement was made, only a few men had been served, yet nearly half our company (which was mostly Catholic) deserted the food line and rushed over to take part in the services, so thankful were the men for being spared.

After dark on the twenty-sixth we received orders to move on—to the front or the rear we did not know. There did not seem to be any rear, for shells appeared to be coming from everywhere; one of them hit a 75 firing from our valley, squarely in the muzzle, destroying the gun and killing the gun crew. After standing in formation for what seemed an interminable time the column began to move. My feet were hurting, I was tired, and we all were weak, starved, sick, emaciated. The column passed out of the Côte des Roches onto the shell-torn highway that paralleled the Meuse, trudged along the winding highway, over hills, through valleys. On the exposed hills the road was screened with camouflage, and on our left the horizon glowed with the flashes of the big guns. These marches were hard; the road was being shelled in places, and for a while we would creep along, then run, halt, run again, creep again, and so on for mile after mile. Word would pass down, "Give way to the right," and then a regiment of artillery or an ammunition train or infantry on the way to the line would pass. The artillery horses were pitiful, reduced to skin and bones. Late in the night we passed the two giant American naval guns that were supposed to be a match for the famous Big Bertha. It seemed that we were not leaving the front but paralleling it, and yet at daybreak we marched into Verdun and halted on the lee side of a range of hills outside the city, where we made ourselves comfortable in dugouts in the hillsides. We were beginning to get a little food and had some grape jelly, butter, and bread, quite a feast. During the day several of us decided to walk around and look over the town, or what was left of it, but we changed our minds when a big shell exploded in the river close by a bridge we were crossing.

On the night of October 28 we left Verdun and marched to Moulin Brule and camped in the same woods the regiment was in when I joined it, occupying the same huts. It was a grand feeling to be sleeping above ground under a roof once more. On the way we passed through several villages deserted by their inhabitants but with a few soldiers of the back area service units occupying some of the houses. As we passed through the dark streets I could see narrow slits of light showing through where blankets were hung over windows and knew the inside was lighted and occupied. I envied those men in a house with the comfort of light and perhaps heat. We were like the animals of the forest, without light or heat and sleeping on the ground in the weather.

At Moulin Brule the military police brought in our deserter first sergeant and turned him over to Grassey. I was not in Grassey's quarters when Murphy was taken in, but I saw him when he came out; he showed signs of having been through the mill. Grassey was capable of handling deserters.[4]

On the night of October 31 we were loaded into camions—French motor trucks—and it seemed that we were going to ride away from the front. It was true; the 29th Division was relieved that night and ordered to the rear to equip and get replacements.[5] We rode four or five hours, quite uncomfortably in the crowded trucks, without headlights, to a village a few miles from Bar-le-Duc, and here the 3d Battalion "detrucked" to occupy billets for the first time since the big battle had begun. The enlisted men occupied barns and the officers occupied rooms in dwellings. Grassey and I occupied the same room and the same bed, and each of us smelled so badly that the other had difficulty going to sleep. Next day we found some water and took our first baths in four weeks.

★ XI ★
AFTERMATH

Not long after the 29th Division had left the line, the Armistice was concluded, November 11, 1918. The war was over.

To men of the division, and to all Pershing's troops of the AEF, the principal concern now became going home and getting out of the army.

No part of service in the army proved so tedious as the months of waiting before taking ship at Brest or St. Nazaire. Soldiers of the AEF believed that Pershing and his officers did not want to give up wartime ranks and authority and hence bedeviled the men by keeping them around. The AEF was in an irritable mood, remembering the thought that inspired them in the autumn of 1918—Hell, Heaven, or Hoboken by Christmas. Pershing inveighed against "relaxation in discipline, in conduct, in appearance, in everything that marks a soldier," and tried to keep his divisions busy with calisthenics, drills, and all manner of schooling. The program produced far more harm than good; men refused to cooperate. They changed Pershing's supposed remark (actually Captain C. E. Stanton made it) in Paris before Lafayette's tomb, "Lafayette, we are here," to "Lafayette, we are still here."

But there was little that Pershing could have done to get the AEF home sooner. Withdrawal of Allied ships from American service after the Armistice, to serve national needs, threw the burden of homeward transit on the U.S. navy, which converted all possible vessels into troopships—cargo transports, battleships, cruisers, ten enemy ships; it expanded the troop fleet to four times its size on Armistice Day, 174 vessels accommodating 419,000 passengers. But 2 million men needed to come home. Most of them had to wait until the spring and summer of 1919.

And yet, once men crowded into the ships, almost like cattle they said, and endured the passage that averaged twelve days, it was all over. The 29th Division's units landed in Hoboken and Newport News in mid-May 1919, and after parades in such localities as Atlantic City—many of the units were from New Jersey—the men received discharges and went home as rapidly as trains and streetcars would carry them.

Douglas Lawrence went home a bit later, with a group of casual officers, and was mustered out at Camp Dix on May 29, 1919.

During our first day in billets in the village near Bar-le-Duc, November 1, 1918, we began to clean up, replace lost and damaged equipment, and fill vacant files with new men. Replacements brought our strength back to normal, numerically speaking, but it took longer to bring back our physical strength. And our recess was to last only ten days. Our higher officers were ruthless in whipping the division back into shape so as to go back to the front on schedule. Indiscipline was not tolerated, and the inclination to take things easy was checked with an iron hand. Officers were called before superiors and severely reprimanded for slight disciplinary infractions. A number of officers were relieved for minor transgressions. In this way we were slapped from after-battle lethargy back to normal efficiency.

Leave was granted under certain conditions to go into Bar-le-Duc, and I was fortunate to be placed in charge of a leave detail of fifteen men selected from the battalion. None of the men had any money, and since I just had received my pay I lent each man twenty francs, about four dollars. I did not bother to take their names, for two hard-boiled sergeants said it was not necessary—they would see that each man paid his when he got it. Every dollar was repaid. Bar-le-Duc was a city of about 15,000 inhabitants, and to visit it was like going to heaven—a haircut, bath, good food, and civilization again. But only for a few hours.

A day or two later I was put in charge of a detail of about a dozen sergeants to visit an airfield near the front for instruction and maneuvers in liaison between the infantry and the air service. We set out on a cold, rainy morning in army trucks without any kind of shelter. I sat on the seat with the driver and we wore our overseas caps, the most useless piece of equipment ever concocted, for they afforded protection against neither rain nor sun; in the rain they would get soggy, and little streamlets would issue from them, down into our eyes and down our necks.[1] I sat on the front seat in the rain and slept in spite of the rain and my overseas cap. I rode in my first plane at the aviation camp, and the maneuver lasted for two days, after which we returned to our regiment. When we returned to our village we saw French flags draped from the windows, and the French said the war was over, but it was not, although there was talk of an armistice.

135

We received orders on November 10, 1918, to be ready to move the next day, to march toward Metz and take part in an assault on that city, regarded as the most fortified position on the Western Front. We were not enthusiastic about another battle, for the last had stripped war of its glory, and we hoped an armistice would be signed. On the morning of November 11, Grassey and I regretfully left our comfortable room in the little French house and with full equipment joined the company formed in the street outside, took our places, and waited the command for the battalion to march. It did not come, and instead we received the command to fall out.

We remained in France about six months after the Armistice, and those were trying months. Discipline was strict and drilling and maneuvers intensive. The men had to be kept busy to keep them out of mischief. But the war was over, and we wanted to go home. We could develop no enthusiasm for the field maneuvers in which we had to take part nearly every day. Many of our officers were relieved because the general did not think they exhibited enough interest in their work. Major General Morton, commanding the division, and Brigadier General Upton, commanding our brigade, became quite unpopular.

Meanwhile we left the village near Bar-le-Duc and moved to another near the town of Passavant, and here Grassey, Derrickson, and I were billeted in the house of a fairly prosperous farmer. We were comfortable, and the meals prepared by the two daughters were good. At this location I was placed in command of the scout and intelligence platoon of the battalion and had to move to battalion headquarters in a neighboring village where my new command of about fifty men was stationed. I enjoyed the assignment, an independent command where I reported only to the major, and kept it for about a month, after which I returned to Company L because of the shortage of officers. The battalion moved to the village of Rozières, about ten miles away, and this was the last move until we went to Le Mans to prepare to embark for home.

At Rozières, I was detailed to the 111th Field Artillery to study artillery tactics, and when I reported to my battery there I was pleased to learn that it was from Norfolk and commanded by Captain John Bentley of Hampton, Virginia. Its other officers were Lieutenants Dustan Armstrong of Norfolk, Rusty Mason of Richmond, and Walter Nolting of St. Paul, Minnesota. I made many friends during my stay with the battery, and learned something about artillery. I was billeted in a very old, allegedly haunted, stone chateau outside the village, and the only other occupant of this dismal building was an old lady who lived downstairs while I occupied one of the numerous rooms upstairs. I was often disturbed by strange goings-on after I had gone to bed, and one night was awakened by the canopy suspended from the ceiling over my bed—the canopy was being violently shaken. I jumped from bed and lit a candle, after some stumbling around, and the shaking stopped, but it started again after I put out the candle and got back into bed. Finally it stopped; I never did find out what it was.

I was sent off on one other temporary assignment, to an infantry officers rifle school for two weeks, and the experience was a grind, although we had fun tormenting our instructors, who had no more heart for the school than we did.

Finally the order came to move to Le Mans, and we were on the way home, for from there we went to the port of St. Nazaire where we stayed two weeks awaiting a ship. While waiting we amused ourselves visiting the

Officers of the 3d Battalion, 113th Infantry, 29th Division, 1919

Officers of the 3d Battalion, poker game in barracks, St. Nazaire, May 3, 1919

interesting surrounding country. When the ship came and we were ready to embark it was found that there were only enough quarters for half the officers, a great disappointment, and it was agreed that the New Jersey officers would have first choice to go with the regiment, so about half the officers, including me, stayed behind. I could hardly keep back the tears as I bade the men of Company L goodbye. I did not know whether I ever would see them again. Some twenty years later, at the end of the 1930s, I did see many of them—a few were doing well, some only fairly so, some were dead, many were derelicts who could not readjust themselves from the shock of war, although some of them would have been derelicts anyway.

We casual officers were transferred to Brest, where we stayed a few days, and then were assigned to part of the 89th Division, which was to embark on the *Prinz Friedrich Wilhelm,* a former German converted cruiser. We sailed about May 18, 1919, it took six days to cross, and we docked at Hoboken.

Several of our party registered at the McAlpin Hotel in New York, and I met my father shortly after arrival; he was a captain in the Medical Corps and had been stationed in New York. I was mustered out at Camp Dix on May 29, and went to Pendleton to see the rest of my family. I did not stay there long, for I was restless. The war had done something to me. And so I decided to go to the University of Virginia and continue my education.

Joseph Douglas Lawrence, Clemson, S.C., 1985 (aet. 90)

NOTES

Chapter One

1. In World War I the entrance of National Guard units into federal service was marked both by renumbering of Guard units and by massive increase in unit size—the latter because of the shortage of trained officers of the Regular Army. The War Department opted for units of extraordinary size: companies of 250 men, four companies to a battalion, three battalions to a regiment (which with supporting troops numbered 4,000); two infantry regiments to a brigade; two infantry brigades and a smaller artillery brigade to a division (which with supporting troops numbered 28,000). Lawrence's company from Florence, Company K, had been part of the 1st South Carolina Infantry Regiment, which upon being taken into federal service became the 118th Infantry. Together with another infantry regiment and the 114th Machine Gun Battalion, the 118th formed the 59th Infantry Brigade. Like other American divisions the 30th Division with its three brigades was markedly larger than British and French divisions, which numbered 10,000-12,000, and virtually equaled a European corps.

2. Sam J. Royall, *History of the 118th Infantry* (Columbia, S.C., 1919), pp. 7-9. Lieutenant Royall had been first sergeant of the National Guard company from Florence and was so popular that the men elected him a lieutenant. Election of officers was the custom in Guard companies.

3. Lawrence D. Tyson, born in 1861, had graduated from West Point in 1883 but resigned from the army in 1896 to enter the practice of law in Knoxville, Tennessee. A colonel of volunteers in the Spanish-American War, he afterward served with the Tennessee National Guard. When the 30th Division was formed partly from Guard units from Tennessee, he received command of the 59th Infantry Brigade. After World War I he became publisher of the Knoxville *Sentinel,* and was U.S. senator from Tennessee from 1925 until his death in 1929 (Samuel C. Williams, "Lawrence D. Tyson," *Dictionary of American Biography* [New York, 1936], vol. 10, pt. 1, pp. 104-5). Before the march into Belgium in early July 1918 he had criticized two battalions of the 117th Infantry and the 2d Battalion of the 118th (Lawrence was in the 3d) for poor march discipline, and this may have had something to do with the pace he set into Belgium. On June 25 he had further admonished regimental commanders and his machine-gun battalion commander, in capital letters, "MARCH DISCIPLINE IS THE CEREMONIAL OF WAR. YOU CAN, IF YOU TRY, MARCH AS WELL AS THE WEST POINT CADETS" ("Transfers, Assignments . . .", box 138, record group 120, National Archives, Washington, D.C.). After the armistice he seems to have forgotten everything, and in General Order no. 1, February 22, 1919, recalled "nothing but loyalty and cooperation and courtesy from each and every officer and man from the time I took command . . . in November, 1917 down to this good hour . . . the spirit of the officers and men during all this time could not have been finer" ("History," box 11, record group 120).

Chapter Two

1. Elmer A. Murphy and Robert S. Thomas, *The Thirtieth Division in the World War* (Lepanto, Ark., 1936), p. 74.

2. John Ellis, *Eye-Deep in Hell: Trench Warfare in World War I* (New York, 1976), pp. 10-12. See also John Keegan, *The Face of Battle* (New York, 1977), pp. 209-215.

3. "I was loafing around an English canteen at Dirty Bucket one day when I engaged in some talk with an elderly English YMCA man, who told me he believed the Allies had lost the war—that the Americans were too late. He pointed to a detail of replacements marching by, that recently had arrived from England, and said, 'Look at those old men and young boys. What can you expect of them in battle?' It was true, of course, that the British were scraping the bottom of the manpower barrel at this time" (original version of Lawrence's memoir, Military History Research Collection, U.S. Army Military History Institute, Carlisle Barracks).

4. The author here changed names of the protagonists. In several places in the narrative he has done likewise.

5. Captain William L. Gillespie, of Cheraw, S.C., commanding Company I of the 118th Infantry.

Chapter Three

1. In the original of his memoir Lawrence was here reminded of Biff Hall, once sergeant of the company, who had misbehaved, "and during the trip across on the *Orduna* it had been necessary to put him in a cage. One night while my platoon was in the front line, two guards passed through our trench with Hall in tow. They carried him to where our line joined the Belgians and where a shell had destroyed the trench, and put him to work repairing the gap. It seemed to me like this was murder, because when we passed the spot, as we did quite often in patrolling this part of the trench, we had to crawl, and if any part of us showed, a German bullet was sure to strike close by immediately. They seemed to have this section under close watch. We had to observe from this section with a periscope. On one occasion I had a German bullet strike within an inch of my periscope. I had an idea that Hall was being put to work here as a good means of getting rid of him. He worked on this gap for several hours, however, and I do not think a bullet was fired at him. Some of the men thought he was in league with the Germans. I can see old Hall

now, silhouetted against the moonlit sky, his unshaven face and huge paws giving him the appearance of a big gorilla."

2. Readers with army service will understand Captain Gillespie's decision to return Hook to the United States. Army procedures often worked contrary to plan.

Chapter Four

1. At Cantigny late in May 1918, American troops fought their first sizable action under their own commanders and took the village that because of its slight elevation had given advantage to the Germans along that part of the front. Hardly had Cantigny been gained than the 2d and 3d Divisions went into action in the vicinity of Château-Thierry. Here the 2d Division's Marine brigade occupied Belleau Wood in the bloodiest encounter in Marine history until Iwo Jima in World War II—5,183 men killed or wounded. The 2d Division's army brigade, together with the 3d Division, held a line at Vaux and along the Marne on the edge of Château-Thierry, and eventually captured both localities. Defeat of a unit of the 26th Division, to which Lawrence refers, was at Seicheprey where in April 1918 the Germans raided trenches held by the "New England Division," a National Guard division; enemy artillery first bracketed the trenches with artillery fire, and assault troops killed eighty defenders and took 130 prisoners.

2. Proven attracted troops, according to the diary of Private Willard M. Newton of the 105th Engineer Train, 30th Division: "Several of us fellows go to Proven in the morning and learn all the latest rumors. This town has a population of about three thousand inhabitants and has not been damaged by shellfire as have the other towns farther toward the front. I stop a while in an estaminet crowded with Belgian and French soldiers and civilians. On the wall is plastered a large notice warning all soldiers not to talk about the movement of troops or to discuss anything of the late happenings at the front, as there may be spies about" (entry of August 11, 1918, Military History Research Collection, U.S. Army Military History Institute).

3. Colonel P. K. McCully of the 118th had recommended Lawrence as early as May 27 ("Personnel series May, 1918," box 8, Lawrence D. Tyson MSS, University of North Carolina Library, Chapel Hill).

4. "Late in the afternoon of the first day we arrived at Eutaps, in France, a British concentration center, and were allowed to leave the train for a half hour. We had had little food since leaving Proven, and the first thing we did was try to find some. We found a British canteen where we were able to buy hot tea and teacakes. The latter were very good and sold two for a penny, and I looked over the canteen's stock of cakes and figured that at the rate of two for a penny I could buy the whole stock for fifteen francs, about three dollars. I therefore offered the British Tommy in charge fifteen francs. He was astounded at such a display of wealth, but managed to regain control and say that his stock was not for sale to speculators. He explained politely that he could sell only ten cakes to one man" (original of Lawrence's memoir).

5. "Fred was from Florence, and from this time on he and I were close friends, not separated for a day until the tide of war turned our steps in different directions some months later."

6. "I was next to the shortest. Miller, of Rockhill, was shortest. Bullock from Newberry, was selected corporal of our squad because he was the tallest of the four in the front rank of the 'runt' squad."

Chapter Five

1. The 42d (Rainbow) Division was one of the first American divisions to reach France. Its units came from many states, and Major Douglas MacArthur had suggested that it be known as the Rainbow Division. Promoted to brigadier general, MacArthur eventually commanded one of its infantry brigades.

2. Charles G. Morton was born in Maine in 1861 and graduated from West Point with the class of 1883. Promoted through the grades to brigadier general in July 1916, he

became a major general in May 1917 when the army raised all its regular brigadier generals to that rank. During his early years he served in frontier forts and was professor of military science and tactics at East Florida Seminary in Gainesville (later the University of Florida) and the Florida State Agricultural College in Lake City. In the Spanish-American War he became lieutenant colonel of a Maine volunteer infantry regiment. After several tours in the Philippines and duty on the Mexican border in 1916, he assumed command of the 29th Division when it was organized out of National Guard units at Camp McClellan, Alabama, on July 6, 1917. "I'll give them discipline such as the National Guard has never heard of before," he said. During the war he became known as "Nosey" because of diligence in seeking out breaches of military discipline or etiquette—perhaps also because of his prominent nose, easily discernible in photographs of the time. After the war he commanded the Hawaiian Department and the IX Corps Area with headquarters at the Presidio in San Francisco. He retired in 1925, and died in 1933 from a tetanus infection following an injury sustained in handling a Fourth of July firecracker (Louis H. Bolander, "Charles Gould Morton," *Dictionary of American Biography,* suppl. 1 [New York, 1944], pp. 564-65). Many years later the colonel of the 115th Infantry, Milton A. Reckord, a major general in World War II, recalled that when the 29th Division went into action in 1918, Morton remained in his headquarters six miles in the rear. When Morton's chief of staff, Colonel Sydney A. Cloman, advised Reckord over the field telephone about how to capture machine-gun nests, Reckord angrily told the colonel he did not know anything from such a distance and should come on up front. Remembering this incident, Reckord nonetheless added that it was fortunate he was dealing with the chief of staff, a good man, instead of Morton who was "not qualified to command a division in battle, but he had sense enough to get sick and go to bed and Sydney Cloman ran the division" (Reckord oral history, Military History Research Collection, U.S. Army Military History Institute; interview by Lieutenant Colonel Bernie Callahan, February 2, 1974, pp. 45-

46; February 17, pp. 7-9; April 12, pp. 3-4). Cloman had served on the general staff in Washington and been military attaché in Russia. At the time of the above interview Reckord was ninety-four years of age. Interestingly, Morton considered Reckord, his critic, as the finest colonel he had ever known; so he told Colonel John M. Palmer, commanding the 58th Brigade (I. B. Holley, Jr., *General John M. Palmer, Citizen Soldiers, and the Army of a Democracy* [Westport, Conn., 1982], p. 366).

3. Lawrence's platoon numbered about twenty-five men (report of operations, Company L, 113th Infantry, by First Lieutenant Charles Grassey, November 3, 1918, *Source Book: Operations of the 29th Division East of the Meuse River, October 8th to 30th, 1918* [Fort Monroe, Va., 1922], p. 56). During the Battle of the Meuse-Argonne the 29th Division was considerably under strength, at 23,900 on September 30 and 19,170 on October 31 (*29th Division: Summary of Operations in the World War* [Washington, D.C., 1944], p. 30).

Chapter Six

1. Holley, pp. 367-68.
2. The Austro-Hungarians proved poor fighters, according to Brigadier General LaRoy S. Upton, commander of Lawrence's brigade, the 57th. "During the past two days we have seen a great many Austrian prisoners streaming by to the rear and about the only expression that can be applied to them is 'dregs of humanity' (letter to "Dear Rob," October 10, 1918, Upton MSS, Minnesota Historical Society, St. Paul). Anticipating an Allied attack, the Germans had brought up the 5th, 28th, and 112th Bavarian Divisions. In reserve were the 27th, 37th, and 106th Austro-Hungarian Divisions. In the 1920s and 1930s the War Department arranged for officers to examine records at the Heeres-archiv at Potsdam and copy materials pertaining to divisions opposite American units; for the 1st and 106th Divisions, mentioned above, see boxes 2-3, entry 313, record group 165, National Archives; for the 5th

Bavarian and 15th German, boxes 135, 160, entry 320. Originals then were lost with destruction of the Heeres-archiv early in 1945.

3. Germonville.

4. "Centimes" apparently was Captain Harold A. Content of the American Red Cross. Along the road near the river the Red Cross had established an aid station for the wounded (John A. Cutchins and George Scott Stewart, Jr., *History of the Twenty-ninth Division* [Philadelphia, 1921], p. 161).

Chapter Seven

1. According to Captain Philip C. McIntyre of Company F, 115th Infantry, "It rained 20 days out of the 22. We ditched our overcoats and blankets before we went over the top at 5 A.M. October 8th and they never did catch up to us. You can imagine the suffering with rain and cold without these coverings, but some of the boys got hold of Dutch blankets and kept somewhat warm at night and in addition we received our share of cooties etc. whose noble efforts left us all warm and busy scratching. Then the mud caked upon us kept out some of the cold" (letter to D. C. Lyle, November 10, 1918, Military History Research Collection, U.S. Army Military History Institute).

2. Millard E. Tydings was born in Maryland in 1890 and after graduating from the Maryland Agricultural College and receiving a law degree at the University of Maryland was elected to the Maryland House of Delegates. After service in World War I he became speaker of the House and was elected to the state Senate, thence to the U.S. House of Representatives, and in 1926 to the U.S. Senate, where he served four terms. A Democrat, he was bitterly assailed by Senator Joseph R. McCarthy of Wisconsin in 1950 and lost his Senate seat. He died in 1961. For service in 1918, Tydings received the Distinguished Service Medal and the Distinguished Service Cross with three citations. Tydings's machine-gun battalion contained four companies, and each regiment of the brigade also had a company, and as brigade machine-gun officer he

thus commanded six companies and seventy-two guns. After World War I he composed a 150-page memoir, part typescript and part manuscript, "The Machine Guns Will . . .," which is now in series II, box 11, Tydings MSS, University of Maryland Library, College Park. Tydings was twenty-eight years old in 1918 and had served on the Mexican border two years before, reenlisted when war broke out, and attended II Corps machine-gun school at Chatillon-sur-Seine. To him the guns made sounds that set them apart from the din of battle—they sounded like "giant typewriters" that went "tack, tack, tack" ("The Machine Guns Will . . .," p 55).

3. Twice wounded, Trestrail refused to leave his command and was killed. His citation for the Distinguished Service Cross read: "When the advance of his company was checked by terrific enfilading fire from machine guns, he halted his men and with great coolness ascended a hill to ascertain the location of the enemy machine-gun nests. He had barely reached the top of the hill when he was killed by an exploding shell" (Cutchins and Stewart, p. 136n).

4. The task of Tydings's gunners was difficult. One man had to carry the gun, another the tripod, and others the ammunition boxes, and they had to lay everything on the ground and assemble it before the gun could fire ("The Machine Guns Will . . .," pp. 85-86). Because the 29th Division's artillery brigade was not serving with the division (below, Chap. 9, n. 7), the machine guns were just about the only artillery support the division had—other than initial support, on October 8, by another artillery brigade. Later during the fighting for the Meuse heights Tydings's machine gunners distinguished themselves in support of the infantry. According to General Upton, "In the attack our movement was parallel to one hill which we held, so my Brigade Machine Gun Officer arranged to put two companies of machine guns on this hill and fired a destructive machine gun barrage parallel to our advancing troops and about 200 meters in front of them. This raised consternation with the Boche and saved us a great many casualties for the Boche could not stand this fire and he beat it and left us many machine guns, fully 60 on

a front of 500 meters. It was a fine chance to employ a machine gun barrage and I am mighty glad that we took advantage of it and got such good results" (letter of October 26, 1918, Upton MSS).

5. During almost the entire action of the 29th Division at the heights of the Meuse, American soldiers received virtually no air cover. German planes machine-gunned troops or acted as spotters for artillery, and did so with impunity. At the outset Allied planes made a dramatic appearance. "Last night I saw a wonderful sight," wrote General Upton. "Four large flocks of wild geese going in the wrong direction, going north. When they got closer I found they were aeroplanes, 122 in the air at one time. It was a wonderful sight and spells the absolute doom of the Boche." But he added that "this is the first air supremacy that I have seen on the Allied side." An hour earlier he had seen a German plane come over and shoot down two observation balloons (letter of October 10). Lawrence seldom saw an American plane, and when one did fly over 29th Division lines the men shot it down. Years later Lawrence by chance met the aviator, who ruefully recalled the experience.

6. Grenades were almost necessary to take machine-gun nests. Second Lieutenant Frank P. Isensee of Company D, 115th Infantry, crawled close to three German guns but could do little: "The only weapon I had was my automatic, but as I could not see any of the machine gunners, it was up to old 'Time' to tell me what to do. I knew now, within two feet's guess, where one of the guns were and the other two by the smoke, I know they were each within 15 or 20 feet from me, in the brushes. If I had only brought me some hand grenades, maybe a present for each gunner, I believe they'd have been fine locators" (letter to D. C. Lyle, November 9, 1918, Military History Research Collection, U.S. Army Military History Institute).

7. American troops at first used machine guns of foreign manufacture, British Lewis guns or the French Chauchat, known as the Sho-Sho, the Sure Shot, or, when it jammed as it regularly did, the Sure something else. In early 1918, U.S.

factories began turning out thousands of Browning automatic rifles and heavy machine guns, best in the world, standard equipment in World War II and the Korean War. General Pershing received 29,000 automatic rifles and 27,000 heavies, but was so proud of them that he did not allow their use on the Western Front until near the end of the war, for fear the Germans would capture and copy them.

8. The 29th Division's history records this encounter (Cutchins and Stewart, p. 165n2).

Chapter Eight

1. When U.S. soldiers trained in the United States they spent much time in bayonet practice, which seems to have had two purposes—to learn how to kill expeditiously, and to give a feel for the ferocity of battle. The second purpose may have been achieved. The first was later much commented upon, for rarely did men in combat use the bayonet. Army surgeons treated few bayonet wounds. The weapons of World War I were pistols, rifles, machine guns, shrapnel, and especially mustard gas.

2. The entire melee described above received but part of a sentence in the 57th Brigade's final report: "Two strong counterattacks against the 113th Infantry, one on the Ravine de Molleville and one on the Ravine de la Reine, were repulsed with heavy losses" (29th Division, "Resume of Action," November 7, 1918, box 8, record group 120). But it was for the action at the Ravine de la Reine that Lawrence was decorated with the Croix de Guerre, by Order no. 12438 "D," December 21, 1918, headquarters, French Army of the East. His company commander, Lieutenant Grassey, collected statements from Corporal Charles Doerfer and Sergeant Lavender, both of Company K. Doerfer related "the splendid example he set for his platoon by rushing forward in the face of enemy fire, and . . . his words of encouragement when we were temporarily halted." Lavender referred to "the bravery and dash, to the splendid and inspiring action, and the fearless leadership." Grassey described "gallantry and leadership in

action against the enemy at Bois de la Reine, France 10th Oct, 1918, in leading his platoon against a nest of seven light Machine Guns manned by about thirty Germans under a severe fire. When the attacking line seemed to waver Lt. Lawrence rushed forward calling to his men to follow him, thereby capturing three guns and killing about twenty Germans, the remainder taking to their heels" ("Efficiency of Officers," folder L 201.1, box 71, record group 120).

3. Lawrence places Sexton's death on October 11. Sexton's citation for the Distinguished Service Cross places it on October 17 (Cutchins and Stewart, p. 165n2). First Lieutenant David W. Paulette wrote Sexton's brother that death occurred "on or about the 19th, day of October, 1918" (letter of January 13, 1919). According to Paulette's after-action report of November 9, 1918, it was October 21 (*Source Book: Operations of the 29th Division . . . ,* p. 59). Unpublished division records likewise put it on October 21 ("Statistical Information," box 140, record group 120). For details of Sexton's death see p. 128. Also the probable reference to Sexton in a German report for October 21-22: "The 32d Division took a prisoner, who died shortly thereafter, however. He belonged to the 118th Infantry of the 30th American Division and had recently been transferred to the 29th American Division" (*German Documents to Accompany Operations of the 29th Division* [Fort Monroe, Va., 1923], p. 532).

4. Whether by night or day, a battlefield was a disorderly place, and certainly no respecter of rank, as General Upton discovered when he went to the front one morning to see his battalion commanders. "I proceed up the narrow gauge railway, every fifty feet a shell has dropped, cutting both rails. Along the road are blankets, cartridge belts, packs, ripped by artillery shell fire. The bearers of these have since been buried. Here is a loaf of bread, there is a half-empty can of salmon; here is a raincoat, here is a pile of packs, ammunition partly broken open, some trampled in the mud. There is a machine gun cart upset, tools and everything missing. Three more dead horses, one shell's toll. Now mustard gas is strong

and I put on my gas mask. I pass a dugout, ask the men what they are doing there; I find two are stragglers and my language to them is violent as I send them on their way back to their Company. Beside the road most all the tree branches are shot off. Here is a water cart, the tank full of holes from one shell. Here is an overturned ammunition cart. I cross the valley, start up a steep hill to the P.C., of a battalion commander. These P.C.'s are on the opposite side of the hills from the French line, of course, now facing the Boche positions. Most of them have three entrances and the Boche is busy shooting them in. He also knows the locations of all the latrines that he has left and he seems to vent his spite on latrines for they are all upset by high explosive shells, and you can guess the rest. The hill is extremely slippery and the soil here is clay. I finally get up to the dugout and squeeze through branches and wire all upset by the last shelling, to get to the entrance. I go down and find the Major, go over the situation with him, cheer him up, take a runner to go to the next battalion P.C., which is further up the hill. As I start back from this place the Boche starts shelling the woods ahead of me, and I leave that behind as I slip and slide down the hill to the valley again. Then I retrace my steps to a valley running east where my second regiment [the 113th, Lawrence's regiment] was badly cut to pieces in its fight two days before. Here is confusion confounded, the floor of the valley is polkadotted with shell craters. I leave the path to try and get better walking, but soon find my feet weighing about six pounds apiece, this due to the lumps of clay I pick up which lie scattered all over the ground from the shell explosions. I come back to the valley because it is easier going. I pass a dressing station. At one side, in a sort of a hole, is a pile of guns, helmets, bayonets, packs, canteens, individual kits,—all the personal belongings of the many wounded which have been taken from them and thrown in a pile. To one side is a low row covered with shelter tent halves. These are the dead, which are yet unburied, for the Boche delights to shoot up burial parties, and some who have been buried have had to be buried over again for shells tear up the ground. These were the young fellows who were so cheerful a day or so before on their way up to get a crack at the Boche" (letter of October 16, 1918, Upton MSS).

5. As Tydings described the scene, "German artillery grows active. They are concentrating on the ravine where our kitchens are located. In five minutes at least fifty shells have been dropped into it. The Germans have seen either some movement there, or the smoke of the kitchens and have guessed the truth. I leave [Colonel] Pope and go down the Valley and to the ravine. It is a ghostly sight. Dead horses are strewn about. . . . Other horses have broken loose. Some are walking about dragging their intestines. . . . The cooks and kitchen force had jumped into the cover of foxholes when the shelling commenced. There was no time to look after the poor horses. The seriously wounded animals are being shot down to take them out of their misery. Less seriously wounded ones are being quieted and led to the rear. Blood and parts of horses are splattered over the kitchens. The sight of food in such a setting fills one with a kind of nausea. Strangely, it seems, I feel more pity for these dead and wounded animals than I would feel if they were human beings" ("The Machine Guns Will . . . ," p. 109).

Chapter Nine

1. Two days before, on October 10, Corporal Stuart had displayed extraordinary heroism and later received the Distinguished Service Cross for leading his squad "under difficult circumstances" to its objective, although the enemy greatly outnumbered them. "Singlehanded he afterward killed six of the enemy and captured two machine guns." Cutchins and Stewart, op. cit., p. 165n1. Lawrence recalled that Stuart "killed one German with the butt of his pistol; he was one of the bravest men I ever saw." Lawrence to his mother, Mrs. Joseph H. Lawrence, October 23, 1921.

2. In a recommendation of November 16, 1918, Colonel Pope excoriated Staley, and General Upton penciled a note, "Capt. Staley is entirely unqualified to command a Co." General Morton relieved Captain Staley on November 24, and

sent him to Blois, the AEF's casual camp for officers. Morton's endorsement was severe: "The reason why you are relieved is because it has been demonstrated that you do not possess the tactical knowledge, the qualities of leadership and the ability to enforce discipline, necessary in a company commander" ("Dismissals," box 79, record group 120).

3. Minenwerfers were German trench mortars.

4. Corporal (Acting Sergeant) William H. Ruddy was "an entertaining fellow, and made my stay on the line with him more bearable with his interesting discourses whispered as he and I lay in the same mudhole. Back at Camp Sevier in South Carolina there was a Captain Wilkinson in our regiment, the 118th Infantry, who commanded a company in this regiment. He had a reputation of being a peculiar man and his company was the poorest disciplined unit in the regiment. Before we left for overseas our National Guard colonel was relieved and the regiment placed under command of a hard-boiled Regular Army officer, Colonel H. A. Pattison, who relieved Wilkinson of his command and caused him to resign his commission.

"Wilkinson took his ouster from the Army very hard, and vowed that he would reenlist as a private and go overseas and regain his captaincy, and we heard later that he had enlisted in some infantry regiment when it was embarking for France. As I was leaving Langres for my assignment after I had been commissioned, I saw Wilkinson coming in with a detachment of sergeants to attend the officers school. Several of us of the 118th spoke to him for a few minutes and learned that he had been with the 29th Division. When Ruddy learned later, while we were in the shell hole, that I was from South Carolina, he told me there had been a curious individual who had left Company L for officers training school a few days before I joined the company; this individual, he said, was from the South and was crazy, and Captain Archer had sent him to the officers school to get rid of him. The man had joined Company L while it was embarking at Newport News, said Ruddy, and his name was Wilkinson and he claimed to have been a captain in a Southern regiment but nobody believed him. It was thought he was a fugitive from justice.

"Ruddy told me several interesting stories about Wilkinson. When the 29th Division was moving into Alsace, Captain Archer had called for a volunteer who could speak French to accompany a sergeant who was to go ahead and arrange for billets for the company, and Wilkinson had volunteered. Ruddy was the sergeant. When he and Wilkinson arrived at the village where they were to arrange for billets, Ruddy discovered to his dismay that Wilkinson could not speak French. Nor could Ruddy. Wilkinson's clumsy attempts to speak French aroused the suspicions of the French authorities and they summarily placed Ruddy and Wilkinson in jail, where they remained for three days until Company L marched in. Of course there were no billets for the company because the billet detail could not speak French and had its field of activity limited to the narrow confines of a jail cell.

"When I returned to South Carolina after the war I learned that Wilkinson had returned to his home, wearing captain's bars and a Croix de Guerre. He could not have won the Croix because after he was commissioned a second lieutenant at the officers training school he was assigned to a division that never went into action" (original of Lawrence's memoir).

5. World War I soldiers frequently went for days with wet feet—it was almost impossible to dry them—and the result was a painful peeling of skin and opening of virtual wounds that incapacitated otherwise able-bodied men. Army manuals advised an extra pair of dry socks, but this recourse availed little in the Meuse-Argonne where autumnal rains soaked the thick woods and turned open hillsides into seas of mud. The shallow trenches of the Meuse campaign were of course wet at the bottom, and seldom had parapets where men could stand above the water. Shell holes pooled or puddled. Leather shoes leaked immediately and stitches rotted, converting shoes into sandals. Rubber boots, seldom available, sweated after a few hours and produced as much trench foot as did leather shoes.

6. At midnight, October 17-18, 1918, the 113th Infantry had an effective strength of thirty-seven officers and 1,214 men (*Source Book: Operations of the 29th Division . . . ,*

p. 355). On October 19 the 3d Battalion had 370 men and nine officers, Company L numbered seventy-seven men and three officers ("Strength Reports," box 8, record group 120). General Upton, born in 1869, graduated from West Point in 1891 and was promoted through the grades to brigadier general in August 1918. He was awarded a D.S.C. for "extraordinary heroism" at Soissons on July 18-19, 1918, and later a D.S.M. and Croix de Guerre with three palms. He died in 1927.

7. Because of the U.S. army's failure to mass-produce an artillery piece of its own, American artillery brigades used the French 75. At the outset War Department ordnance officers could have mass-produced its gun of 1902, which was as good as or better than the 75, but failed to see that gun's advantages. Perhaps wisely, they chose not to adopt a piece that became available in 1916, known to critics as the Crime of 1916. But when they adopted the French 75 and sought to mass-produce it from blueprints, the French piece's rigid tolerances—artisans had produced it—delayed deliveries until too late. In the event the French equipped the AEF with 1,828 75s, all that Pershing requested. Unfortunately American artillerymen had to train with those guns in France, and one result was commitment of divisions such as the 29th without its artillery regiments—the 29th's were in training and never got into action. Lawrence and his men badly needed artillery support. Lacking experience in combat, American artillerists may also have failed to sense the infantry's need for far more artillery support than army doctrine advised. Major General Charles P. Summerall, eventually one of Pershing's corps commanders and the army's leading artillery expert in the field, estimated after the war that efficient artillery preparation required far more guns than the AEF ordinarily used. "The war has . . . repeatedly demonstrated that any position, however strong, can be neutralized and captured, with a sufficiently powerful fire, and that invariably the lack of sufficient superiority of fire is paid for in losses to the infantry and even in failure" ("Study on

Organization, Armament and Employment of Artillery," January 4, 1919, AEF files, record group 120).

Chapter Ten

1. The 26th (New England) Division, which suffered the German trench raid at Seicheprey, may not have been at fault on that occasion, as any front-line troops were vulnerable to such raids if attackers used sufficient force. But later, in the Battle of Soissons that opened July 18, when 75,000 American troops under French command pushed in a large German salient that reached to the Marne by attacking its western side and eventually capturing Soissons, the 26th Division did not do well. During the Meuse-Argonne, Pershing and his field commander, Lieutenant General Hunter Liggett, were furious with the commander of the 26th, Major General Clarence R. Edwards, a Regular Army officer beloved by his men, because Edwards lost an infantry brigade for three days. The 26th was a National Guard division weak in field-grade officers, and Edwards ran it without the taut control necessary to keep such a sizable force going. Pershing relieved Edwards in October, using the pretext that the army needed him back in the United States to train troops.

2. Lieutenants Bailey and Running both received the Distinguished Service Cross posthumously, Bailey for "extraordinary heroism in action near Verdun, France, October 12, 1918. Leading his platoon against an enemy position, Liet. Bailey was fatally wounded but refused to leave until his position was organized and a counterattack repulsed." Running's citation was likewise extraordinary heroism the same day—"While advancing on an enemy position under direct machine-gun fire, he was seriously wounded but remained with his platoon until he died" (Cutchins and Stewart, p. 177n1).

3. If the 29th Division commander, Major General Morton, was far behind the lines, the commander of the 57th Brigade was not: Brigadier General Upton placed his command post in the Côte des Roches, "at all times under fire from the

enemy's artillery. During the time the P.C. was here two casualties were sustained . . . 2 horses were killed and 5 wounded by shell fire" ("Resume of action," November 7, 1918, box 8, record group 120). As Upton himself described the location, "Yesterday afternoon at 1:00 o'clock the Boche decided that where we were located would be a good place for a Brigade P.C., and they shelled us all the afternoon and a good part of the evening. Fortunately I had picked out the reverse slope of a hill where the slope of the ground was too great for shells to come down, so they either hit at the top of the hill or at the bottom just beyond us, and they hit both to the right and to the left of us, but fortunately no one of my Brigade Detachment of 90 officers and men were touched" (letter of October 13, 1918, Upton MSS). And again: "Last night I turned in in my dugout good and tired. Early this morning I was awakened by a terrific crash as a shell strikes near the entrance, and soon we have to put on our gas masks because of the phosgene. The bombardment continues and after we dress and go down to the office we find that four men have been killed 100 yards to the east, and one of our horses is killed. This afternoon the Boche opened up on us again at 4:00 o'clock and as we stand there listening to the shells light all around, one drops 150 yards beyond us and kills one of three men who are passing along the road as we look at them" (letter of October 14). "I have a telephone in my dugout, but the wire is frequently shot out between it and my telephone central at the foot of the hill" (letter of October 23).

4. Sergeant Murphy may have escaped military justice. Before a general court martial he pleaded not guilty and was acquitted. The record was twice sent back for revision, but the court refused to change it. On December 13, 1918, the division chief of staff, by then Colonel Clarence O. Sherrill, disapproved the acquittal ("G.C.M.O. #11 to #15, Dec. 1918," box 169, record group 120). The records do not reveal what happened thereafter.

5. Total division casualties in the Meuse-Argonne were 5,006, of which thirty-nine were for October 2-7, 4,081 for October 8-22, and 886 for October 23-31. The 113th

Infantry had no losses for October 2-7; eighty-eight killed, thirty died of wounds, 425 wounded for October 8-22; and thirty-nine killed, seven died of wounds, 126 wounded for October 23-31 (totals of 127 killed, thirty-seven died of wounds, 557 wounded) (*29th Division: Summary of Operations in the World War,* p. 28).

Chapter Eleven

1. In World War I the original issue of hats, apart from metal helmets, was the traditional broad-brim of the Regular Army and National Guard, the hat of the Spanish-American War, which may have made its initial appearance on the Western plains during campaigns against the Indians. For some reason the AEF abandoned the broad brims—doubtless easily mashed in troop trains or aboard ship. Pershing may have desired to distinguish AEF soldiers from men at home, similar to the distinction he made for AEF officers—the Sam Browne belt. For a while some overseas soldiers managed to keep their "campaign hats." According to Private Newton of the 30th Division, "In the afternoon we are issued overseas caps, but we still keep our campaign hats. These caps are known as the 'go-to-h--l' caps. They keep neither the sun nor the rain out of one's face. They can be worn under the helmet or put in the pocket of the trousers when at the front" (Diary, July 5, 1918). The division commander on July 23 ordered all remaining campaign hats to salvage and charged military police to arrest men wearing them ("July 21-25, 1918," box 5, Tyson MSS).

INDEX

161